Girl, Get Your Money Straight!

Girl, Get Your Money Straight!

*A Sister's Guide to Healing
Your Bank Account and Funding
Your Dreams in 7 Simple Steps*

Glinda Bridgforth

BROADWAY BOOKS
New York

Disclaimer

Many of the names and identifying characteristics of the individuals depicted in this book have been changed to protect their privacy. Some of the individuals described are composites of two or more people.

BROADWAY

Broadway Books titles may be purchased for business or promotional use or for special sales. For information, please write to: Special Markets Department, Random House, Inc., 1540 Broadway, New York, NY 10036.

BROADWAY BOOKS and its logo, a letter B bisected on the diagonal, are trademarks of Broadway Books, a division of Random House, Inc.

ISBN 0-7679-0487-7

Designed by Erin L. Matherne and Tina Thompson

To my parents, Walter and Opal Bridgforth.
With love and appreciation.

Contents

Acknowledgments

I believe every person I've ever crossed paths with has influenced my life in some way. They have all helped to make me the person I am, which enabled me to write this book. However, I am eternally grateful to some specific people:

To those whose support and encouragement led me to take on this project as they paved the way before me: Brenda K. Wade, Ph.D., Cheryl D. Broussard, Brooke M. Stephens, Gail Perry-Mason, Kelvin Boston, Fran Harris, George Fraser, and Maria Denise Dowd. A special thank-you to Susan L. Taylor, who has taught me more than she'll ever know. Also, heartfelt thanks for giving me opportunities to share my knowledge and experience with *Essence* readers.

Thank you to the dynamic sisterfriends who reminded me how close I was to the finish line on the manuscript and for all the times they said no when I called to ask for permission to quit: Brenda J. Allen, Ph.D., Denise Barnes-Wiley, Dorothy Hood, Karen James, Jewel Kittell, Charmaine McClarie, Jwahir Moore, and Vivian Jenkins Vanderwerd. Thanks Lisa Patton for your encouragement, ongoing assistance, and for giving me the word "straight." To my focus group participants for being such a great sounding board: Revola Austin, Wendy Fay Baines, Greer Collins, Sheila Griffie, Michelle Lewis, Sheila Thomas, Kimberly Winston, and Vaneese Johnson. And thanks to other friends who came through when I needed them: Rahman Batin, Benay Curtis-Bauer, Piper Douglas, Marjorie Grace, Harriet Y. Wright, Charles Motte, Jr., Timothy E. McDaniel, Ed Rau, Charles Rivers, Danita Rowden, and Joycelyn Thompson.

Many thanks to Bonnie Solow, my literary agent, who read the very early drafts of this book and continued to believe in me anyway. To Lauren Marino, executive editor at Broadway Books, who helped me see the greater vision. And to the wonderful editors who came to my rescue at various stages: Brenda Lane Richardson, Susan McHenry, and Mary Ellen Butler. A special thank-you to Ann Campbell, my extremely talented Broadway Books editor, whose energy and enthusiasm kept me writing when I felt there were no more creative thoughts or ideas in my body.

I lovingly give thanks to my family. My dad, Walter B. Bridgforth, who gave me the courage to venture out twenty-five years ago when he said, "If things don't work out for you in California, you can always come home"; to my mom, Opal Bridgforth, who inspired my book title when she'd call me in California and greet me with an endearing, melodic, "Hey, girl." It was always so special. Thank you to my sisters, who are beautiful and unbelievably generous: Barbara Norwood for being the first super-talented female I admired as she sang, played piano, and directed the choir at New Mt. Herman Baptist Church when she was still a teenager; Doris Saulsberry for being my role model for academic excellence and opening her home to me during the Kalamazoo years; Yvonne Morrison for her fabulous fashion sense and always keeping the boutique open for me; Paula Bridgforth for her selflessness and willingness to carry the ball (I really appreciate you!); and to my sister Ann Lewis for welcoming me with open arms and for the many years of loving support. To my brother, Walter B. Bridgforth, Jr., a special acknowledgment and thank-you for things too numerous to mention here. He's the best man I ever met, and I know there's a place waiting for him in heaven.

Thank you to my sister-in-law, Anita Baker Bridgforth, for being the role model for talent, hard work, and success. Also for her support and guidance during times when I felt challenged by the creative process. To my brothers-in-law: Joe Lewis, for reminding me of my "thin" days; Robert Norwood, for the "meanest" greens I've ever eaten; Van Morrison for the prayer by telephone which he's probably forgotten; and Darrell Saulsberry, for being such a great assistant at my Atlanta seminars. To my nieces, who are talented and smart: Sharon Bridgforth, Yvette Simpson, Kimberly Dart, Stephanie Saulsberry, Tracey Saulsberry, and Sonja Perryman. To my nephews-in-law, Victor Simpson and Elgin Dart, for the many positive words. Thank you to the youngest men in the family, who make me laugh and bring me incredible joy, my nephews, Lil' Walt, Eddie, and Justin. Many thanks to my aunt, Shirley Moore, for opening her heart and her California home to me. To my cousins, Tracey Moore-Marable and Sheila Lavender, for all of the encouraging phone calls; to my Deacon Street surrogate parents, Callie Baker, Andrew and Mattie Fritz, Jack and Fannie Kennedy, the late Laura Cooper, Ethel Smith, and Florence Allison for fostering such a strong sense of community; and to my homegirls Jackie Kennedy, Joan Baker Hill, Andrea Fritz, Darlene Cooper Jordan, and Karen McCary Willis for over forty years of true friendship.

Finally, my sincere thanks to the many participants at my workshops, and a heartfelt thank-you to my clients, past and present, whom I love dearly. I value having the opportunity to work with you and am grateful that many of us have become wonderful friends. So, for all of those who kept asking, "How's the book coming?" here it is. Enjoy.

Girl, Get Your Money Straight!

 *Part One*

Preparing
Your Mind for
Financial Success

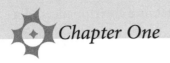 *Chapter One*

The Road to
Financial Healing

Whether you are one of those sisters who owe more than they own, or you are scuffling to make ends meet on a solid income that would make your mama's jaw drop and say, "Girl, you make *how much* money?" believe this: We can *all* learn to shrink our debt, expand our investments, and cultivate financial health, wealth, and peace of mind.

Believe me, I know this is true. The publication of *Girl, Get Your Money Straight!* marks my twenty-fifth year as a financial professional. After a successful career as a retail-banking executive, I have worked for the last decade as an independent consultant, coaching sisters just like you and me through the often tricky waters of money management. I call myself a financial recovery specialist, highly experienced in helping clients who are financially challenged in a variety of ways. I assist them in designing and implementing a personalized program of debt reduction and planned spending to stabilize their finances, dig themselves out of familiar money and credit traps, and ultimately build up savings to invest for their futures.

While I have worked with hundreds of clients from all ethnic backgrounds and walks of life, I have been astonished by the number of eager black women who have flocked to my popular group workshop, Money Management: Achieving Prosperity and Debt-Free Living. In 1994 I presented this workshop for the African American Women on Tour Conference, and a standing-room-only crowd of more than two hundred African American women of all ages showed up at an Oakland hotel, ready to learn the strategies and techniques that would help them get their money straight and foster true financial healing. They brought enough energy into that room to light up the whole city, and it was a beautiful sight to behold.

I stood before that audience as a money-management expert, but just as important, as a sister. As an African American woman, I know firsthand our hunger for straightforward financial information that directly connects with how we live, the feelings we have about ourselves, how we interact with the world at large, and the dreams we want to realize.

I also stood before that audience as a firsthand testament to the powers of change that lie within each and every one of us. I am not the kind of financial expert who has *always* had it all together in my own financial life. I've dealt with many of the challenges typically faced by upwardly mobile African Americans who have come of age since the 1970s. Having benefited from access to education and job opportunities most of our parents didn't have, I am part of a generation of African Americans whose buying power is expected to exceed $533 billion in 2000, up from $350 billion in 1990. That's a 70-percent increase over the last decade! But access to larger incomes doesn't automatically bring the confidence and knowledge it takes to manage money well and turn it into wealth. Some of us grew up poor or were raised by folks who grew up with very little and unwittingly passed on to us high levels of insecurity, self-criticism, and self-doubt in all areas of our lives—especially in finance. And like many Americans, once we have money in our pockets, many of us quite innocently get caught up in our capacity to consume. Eventually, we find ourselves bogged down by overwhelming debt and bad credit habits that have been fueled by psychological vulnerabilities that undermine our confidence to control our financial lives.

I help clients, as I once had to help myself, to examine and work through the close link between how we feel about ourselves in relation to money and how effectively or ineffectively we manage our financial lives. Since both psychological and practical barriers prevent us from moving beyond compulsive spending to planned spending and conscious wealth building, I have found that a holistic approach—that is, one that incorporates both the emotional and the practical and works to heal the individual as well as her bank account—best facilitates change. Such an approach worked for me during my own financial recovery, and I've since found that it works for the hundreds of clients I've seen in my practice and in the workshops I've conducted over the last ten years. Taking a close look inside our minds and hearts is often the key to taking control of our fiscal responsibilities.

The Psychology of Money Management

In the 1970s feminists first called attention to the source of a common pattern in women's financial behaviors—a pattern of passivity and doubt in our ability to take control because of childhood socialization as females. We have commonly been taught and encouraged to leave to men any issues relating to power—specifically control of money. A popular statement was "Oh, don't worry your pretty little head about such things." Psychologist Phyllis Chesler in her 1976 book *Women, Money and Power* explored women's attitudes, values, and ultimately our habits and actions regarding money in relation to our training and life experience. This social-psychological perspective struck a responsive chord with many people, but not until the 1990s were these psychological insights adopted widely by mainstream financial experts and used to help the general consumer. National bestsellers like *Your*

Money or Your Life by Joe Dominguez and Vicki Robin and *The 9 Steps to Financial Freedom* by Suze Orman are two excellent examples of very helpful books that use this approach.

People of all races and both genders are products of distinctive cultural histories and family messages that are passed on from generation to generation. These familial and social expectations influence the capabilities, competence, and expectations we have for ourselves in all areas of our lives. Black women, even though we have a longer collective history in the paid labor force than white women, may be especially weighted down by negative messages from our families and the larger society regarding both our personal and economic status, so it's hardly a coincidence that our financial affairs often mirror an underlying personal sense of inadequacy. In actuality, black women today are the products of generations of resourceful women and men who held their families together with little support—material or otherwise—and despite a lot of economic deprivation. But too often society calls attention to our historically degraded social status rather than our triumphs over it.

If we're going to get our money straight, we must become aware of various kinds of emotional conditioning and how we act it out in our financial lives. Perhaps black women more than anyone else can benefit from a holistic approach that addresses our commonplace emotional conflicts. Of course, there are many African Americans who do not struggle with money issues and who have perfectly healthy spending and saving habits. But those of us who do overspend are often caught up in an unconscious attempt to make ourselves feel acceptable in a world that often seems to be working against us.

In a society in which financial status is an important part of what makes people "successful," spending often becomes a means of self-affirmation. But spending to make ourselves feel better—to feel as though we have a certain place in the world—can actually trap us in a downward spiral: The more shame we feel over mounting debts and finances that are not as we'd like them to be, the more paralyzed we become, even prone to depression. And the worse we feel, the more we spend. Ultimately, our money woes can feel like a festering wound that never heals. Consider the following stories of two sisters who found themselves in a dangerous cycle of feel-good spending and debilitating debt.

Living Beyond Your Means

A typical client is Felicia, who at twenty-seven is challenged by the most important mental hurdle in controlling finances: setting priorities and making choices. Five years out of college, she landed a dream job as a marketing communications assistant in a cosmetics company. But despite its glamorous aura, the entry-level job pays only $27,000 a year. That doesn't go very far in covering her average monthly expenses of about $2,100. Her monthly take-home pay: $1,640. She has been living in the red and falling in deeper.

A young single woman with no children, Felicia loves to travel and has taken a big trip almost every year since college. She financed trips to Paris and Jamaica by using her rent money, after which she spent months juggling her other bill payments, scrambling to play catch-up. Delinquent payments severely affected her credit standing. Today she takes cash advances on her Visa just to buy transit cards to get to and from work.

The Secret Spendthrift Syndrome

My client Corliss, a vibrant and youthful forty-six-year-old sister who wears attractive baby dreadlocks, is blessed with an annual income of $57,000 and had $8,000 in debt. Her income puts her in the top 2 percent of African American women earners, and her debt burden isn't outrageously high. Still, Corliss shifted uncomfortably in her chair all through our first session. Other than a small 401K retirement savings plan, she had no significant assets. She was renting her apartment, leasing her car, and although she considered herself a homebody and no big-time spender, her paycheck barely covered her total expenses. She didn't know where her money was going and was afraid she wouldn't have enough to live on after retirement.

While she presented a confident image to the world, she admitted, "I'm very embarrassed by my financial situation. I'm forty-six years old, but I feel like a little child. Up until now I've never been willing to face my finances because it felt so uncomfortable. I just figure if I look good, everybody will think I'm okay. I've got tons of clothes, and it feels really good to shop. But usually by the time I get home I feel terrible and get an awful headache. It's a vicious cycle and I'm stuck in it. What's wrong with me?"

If you, like Corliss and Felicia, haven't yet been able to set a sound course for growth, don't worry—this book gives you the tools you need to identify destructive money patterns and take charge of your home economics. I know that you can do it—because I did. More than a dozen years ago I was burned-out by a high-powered banking career and by a marriage that wasn't working. My finances, too, were running out of control. As I worked to get my life back on track, I came to understand how not feeling worthy and not loving yourself can create patterns of money misuse, leaving us prone to compulsive spending to salve our insecurities. I believe that understanding these potential connections not only promotes health and healing for people suffering from acute financial problems, it can also be a source of valuable insight—an instructive preventive measure even—for many who never fall prey to serious binge spending and the like. We can learn how to avoid sabotaging our own financial security and use the same insights to increase our options for building wealth—whether or not we ourselves are actually secret spendthrifts. I share my own story as a case in point.

My Financial Roots

I am proud to be from Detroit—the Motor City. That's where I was born and where my parents raised their family of six children from 1945 through 1980, always working hard to make ends meet and to educate us for the greater opportunities they expected we would have. The fourth in line, I was a teenager in the 1960s, when the Motown sound dominated radio airwaves and emanated from every Friday- or Saturday-night house party in those days of "blue lights in the basement." It was a magical time. The auto industry was booming, and many folks we knew who worked for the car factories drove shiny new Pontiac Bonnevilles, Buick Electra 225s, and even the ever-popular Cadillac Eldorado. Meanwhile, Berry Gordy, former auto-worker-turned-impresario, built his Motown label by tapping into talented local singers and musicians seasoned in our churches, community centers, and record hops. My homegirls and I would change up weekly on the girl groups we imitated—The Marvelettes, Martha and the Vandellas, the Supremes. Then there were guy groups we swooned over—Smokey Robinson and the Miracles, the Four Tops, and, of course, the "Tempting" Temptations.

I grew up thinking our family was pretty much average and middle class. I knew we weren't poor, because I saw families in my southwest Detroit neighborhood who had much less than we did. We owned our home, always had plenty to eat, dressed pretty well, periodically went south on vacation to visit relatives, and even bought a new car every few years. I also knew there were other kids who had much more than we had—more clothes, larger homes, better cars, and vacations in places I hadn't heard of.

But I had no concept of real wealth and was well into adulthood before I realized that my family was not middle class. At best, we were a striving blue-collar family, and my hardworking parents struggled to give their children what middle-class comforts and security we had— Dad by holding several jobs and Mom by vigilant household management to stretch the money as far as she could.

I can't remember a time when my dad didn't work at least two jobs to support us all. He had a full-time job as a steelworker in a local plant. It was tough and dirty work: The hot air at the plant was filled with soot, and Dad put in eight-, twelve-, and sometimes sixteen-hour shifts. But while putting in thirty-six years at the steel mill, he also held down part-time jobs as a custodian, working ten years at one position and twenty-two years at another.

Mom toiled long hours too, keeping our home spotless, preparing meals, and managing her brood. She also did occasional domestic work in the homes of middle-class white folks and later earned a few extra dollars as a lunchroom attendant at the neighborhood elementary school. But because she was so busy running our large household, she was largely dependent upon my father for financial support.

My parents shared a strong work ethic, and I know they struggled to meet their obligations, but they always had good credit. My dad told me recently that creating excessive debt was never an issue for him because he knew "it was not hard to get credit, just hard to pay it back." Ironically I didn't grasp the substance of that message until I was in my mid-thirties.

I feel incredibly grateful when I think of what my parents endured over the years to provide the best they could for their family. It took extraordinary courage and sacrifice, and the effort left them little time or energy for emotional nurturing or close attention to building their children's self-esteem. I don't particularly remember their saying "I love you" or "I'm proud of you," but I know my folks nurtured me the best they could.

And certainly my basic needs were met, along with many of my wants. I remember one incident from my childhood that illustrates how well I was taken care of. When I was about four years old, I begged and pleaded for an umbrella of my own. At last, in total exasperation, my parents relented, though my mother said to my father, "What's this child going to do with the umbrella when she gets it?" Dad replied, "Just put her coat on and let her stand outside in the rain." Well, that's exactly what they did. I was blissfully happy standing alone in the backyard with my raincoat, boots, and my very own umbrella! Looking back, I recognize that this was the real way my parents showed their love for me—not just by buying me something I longed for, but also by creating an entire experience around it.

Challenging Times in Our Household

But my father also felt the pressures of living, working, and providing for his family during the days of widespread racial segregation and discrimination. These circumstances understandably contributed to a certain amount of stress in my father's life. I often felt we had to walk on eggshells around Dad. Always having to assess his condition or mood was nerve-wracking, and I dreaded the drama and chaos of his occasional unpredictable outbursts.

One time I asked Mom to take us away to where we could have some peace. She responded sympathetically but said realistically, "Where can we go? There's no place I can take all of you kids. I don't have any money. We have to stay here." Fortunately, my mother coped, and our family endured. By the late 1960s, all but two of the kids had moved out on their own, significantly decreasing the pressure on Dad, the breadwinner. He gradually mellowed out. Today, my parents are retired, and they are rather laid-back people with wonderful senses of humor that blossomed, it seems to me, after my siblings and I grew up. They take great delight in visits from their children and grandchildren. Dad has watched so many cartoons with his grandsons that he now says, "I kinda like watchin' 'em." Needless to say, he's a much more relaxed man than he was during my childhood.

But as I grew older, I never forgot that conversation I had with Mom about her inability to leave home and take us with her. I understood her economic dependence on my father, and I was determined not to place myself in a similar situation. At age eight I made a decision always to be in control of my money and my life. I never wanted to be without my own resources or trapped in a difficult living situation with no place to go for support. At least, that was my plan. Little did I realize that as a well-paid, independent, professional woman, I could create other financial traps for myself.

My Upwardly Mobile Path As a Young Professional

Always an excellent student, I majored in education and earned a bachelor of science degree from Western Michigan University. I always knew that I would teach one day, but I had no way of knowing that my true subject matter would grow out of my own very personal triumphs and losses as well as my professional training.

I got my first exposure to the financial-services field working at a credit union and for a finance company during my college years. I was hired into a bank-management-trainee program after graduation, and in 1976 began a twelve-year career with a major California bank. I always felt I had to exceed my bosses' expectations in the workplace, because I knew all too well that black folks have to be better than average to remain employed in corporate America, let alone ascend the corporate ladder. Even with affirmative-action programs and equal opportunity employment, we contend with the residual legacy of the "last hired, first fired" practices blacks lived with during the pre–Civil Rights era. Ultimately I rose to assistant vice president and successfully managed a $90-million unit with twenty-two employees. I was recognized within the bank a number of times for outstanding achievements in retail management. The responsibilities I had for increasing income and reducing expenses while motivating staff and working with customers on checking, savings, loans, and other banking services actually provided me with the foundation for the financial recovery methods I teach now.

During my first years at the bank, I was only dimly aware of the subtle yet pervasive discrimination that black women and men face in the corporate workplace. Still, I always felt somewhat like an outsider within management circles of white men, and I had no mentors or advocates within the company who could make my way up through the ranks any easier. "I do a good job here," I thought, "but I just don't quite fit in with these people."

I have one particularly vivid memory of frustration during my many years at the bank: Once, while discussing with my white supervisor two job offers I wanted to make to potential employees, he suggested I offer a higher salary to the white female candidate, who was right out of college, and a lower salary to the black woman, who not only had a college degree but also two years of experience. Although he may have had some unstated reason to justify the wage disparity, I felt insulted at having to respond tactfully to what I perceived to be blatant unfairness. Luckily, the final decision was mine, and I hired the sister at the appropriate salary—a small victory I quietly cherished.

But difficult daily struggles against inequality continued around me. Unfortunately, I had no one to look out for fairness in my salary increases when I became a manager. Years after I triumphantly hired that sister at a just salary, I was caught by surprise when a white female executive mentioned in passing to me that my own salary was lower than those of white male managers. I don't know whether they had comparable experience, but it's interesting to note that according to United States Department of Labor statistics, as late as 1996 black women earned 62 cents for every dollar earned by white men.

Investing in Love

While I moved ahead in my career, in my private life as a single black woman I was concerned—as were many of my sisters—about the shrinking pool of eligible black men available to me, with increasing numbers dating outside of their race or falling prey to drugs and the criminal justice system. Still, I was to meet and marry the man of my dreams during this period of my greatest career growth.

Let's call him Jeffrey. I know it sounds trite, but the man who is now my former husband really was tall, dark, and handsome—an ex–professional baseball player with a lot of personal charisma. By the time we met he was an experienced sales executive turned entrepreneur with grand ambitions for wealth and independence. Jeffrey was the first man I dated who seemed to know his purpose in life—he believed he could be financially independent and could help others acquire great wealth in the process. Raised in the South during the Civil Rights Movement, he had seen enormous change take place in his lifetime and had his own visions of making a positive contribution to the planet by creating black millionaires using a network marketing system.

So Jeffrey and I shared common personal and professional goals, and his dreams and visions for the future profoundly resonated with my own. After a year of dating we decided to live together. Jeffrey worked his fledgling business full-time, and I worked part-time with him, using my full-time banking salary to support us. We later married and, like other couples, began to build an economic framework for our life together: We established joint credit and bought property. But over the next eleven years, we evolved from a healthy partnership into unhealthy codependence: My primary focus in life became what Jeffrey wanted and needed to the exclusion of my own ambitions and happiness. Ultimately, I became so absorbed in his concerns that I no longer could identify, articulate, or resolve my own. In hindsight, I can see how much of my self-esteem I invested in my ability to please my husband. As we'll discuss in the next chapter, this is a very common mistake made by women in relationships, and for black women who have even more at stake, the consequences can be doubly devastating.

Living in "Virtual Prosperity" to Maintain an Image of Success

To be fair, the seeds of my financial problems had been planted long before I met Jeffrey. For years, I had stable employment as a bank executive, earned a good income, and maintained good credit, my own apartment, and a car. Still, I was living paycheck to paycheck instead of creating a comfortable life below my means.

For several years, the direct sales business that Jeffrey owned—and in which I later became a partner while still maintaining my banking job—didn't grow in the way we'd hoped. I persevered because I truly believed in both him and the business idea. But one day I gave Jeffrey an ultimatum: Either he made his business produce more income or he needed to get other employment. He eventually took a commissioned sales job and made a promising start. But we were very influenced by a watchword heard frequently in our circle of associates: "If you want to achieve something, you have to act as if you already have it." For us that meant "If you want to be financially successful, you must spend as if you already are." The focus of our ill-advised spending became not wealth-building per se, but creating the image of success.

The 1980s were a time of "virtual" prosperity for us. Virtual because our lifestyle was mostly financed by debt and numerous preapproved credit cards with high limits. Nonetheless, our capacity to consume made us feel like we had arrived. Our newfound spending power was so exciting that we were on a high as we shopped without concern for price tags. If we wanted something, we simply charged it. For vacations, we didn't just book a cruise, we traveled in deluxe suites. Once, when all the suites were booked, our travel agent managed to get us the "owner's suite," which was very much like a luxury condo. We even held a cocktail party there, entertaining other couples on board. That pumped us up for a long time. We were making good money, but we were also caught in a vicious cycle; the more we made, the more we wanted—and the more we spent. We had lots of fun, but the reality was that we were broke, although we certainly looked good.

If Jeffrey wanted something and I thought it would make him happy, I found a way to make it happen. We acquired high-end electronics, rental property, and a house in the Oakland hills with spectacular views of San Francisco Bay. Although we had acquired all these "things," they never seemed quite enough—not for Jeffrey and not for me. Still, despite growing discontent and increasing debt, it never occurred to me that my husband and I wouldn't be together forever.

The Time Bomb Explodes: A $50,000 Debt Burden

Our combined income by the mid-1980s was nearly $100,000, which was not too bad. I had always managed our household money, paid the bills, and maintained our bank accounts. But over the years, our reckless spending led to a whopping $50,000 in unsecured debt (i.e., money that was owed to institutions or individuals with no collateral attached) through credit cards, lines of credit, and personal loans.

I continued making a good salary at the bank, but because of the heavy debt burden, I found myself sinking into a sea of financial obligations without a life raft. I had failed miserably at the commitment I made to myself at age eight to control my money and my life and was now in a situation similar to my mom's, feeling hopeless, with nowhere to go for help and financial support.

It's not as though there weren't signs all along the way that our finances were headed downhill. Things had been incredibly tight for a long time. We had arranged several debt-consolidation loans, combining all our credit-card balances into one loan that usually resulted in a lower monthly payment. There had been a slow payment here or there, maybe even a creditor telephone call every now and then. But it didn't come to a head until there was an unexpected break in a sewer line on our income property that would cost $8,000 to repair. This enormous nonoptional sewer expense was terrifying because it added pressure beyond the tipping point. This is how I came to see that our financial situation was completely out of control.

I took charge, got creative, and found a way to deal with the situation. I obtained a hardship withdrawal from my 401K plan at work to repair the sewer problem. But while that solved our immediate crisis, it didn't help our general finances. Besides, there was growing trouble in the marriage. Jeffrey had become emotionally distant and it seemed we'd come full circle; I once again carried the majority of the financial burden in the household—except now our debt was huge and unmanageable.

By this time it was 1988, and I was still with the bank, not only as manager of the operation but covering three other positions as well, because I had lost key staff members. Not able to fill those positions immediately, I shouldered the extra load. I found myself working from seven A.M. to seven P.M., plus another two or three hours when I got home at night. I was running hard on a treadmill and falling farther and farther behind. I asked my supervisor for additional hands, but his reply was "I don't have anyone available to help you, and I can't lower your goals. Keep your staff motivated and do the best you can." Had I been a white manager, I wondered, would I have received more assistance? But needless to say, I had to play the cards I'd been dealt, and soon I was simply burned out. As a friend of mine puts it, "I was so burned, I was crispy!"

It's hard to forget the tremendous dismay I'd feel each morning as I got in my car to begin the twenty-minute drive to my office. Tears would stream down my face as I rolled through the streets of Oakland. Trying to blink them back, I wondered, What happened here? I used to love my job, and even though it's always been a challenge, I used to enjoy that aspect of it. Now it's just not fun anymore.

I remember working with a client on bank approval for a $100,000 line of credit. His paperwork was in order and I was confident it would be approved. But when the loan department granted him only $50,000, I completely lost it. I broke down and cried on the telephone with the loan officer! This was not my personal application, but I took my client's lower credit limit as my personal failure, and I felt worthless.

Stunned by my own reaction, I turned to the employee assistant department to discuss my uncharacteristic, unprofessional behavior regarding the customer's loan approval. After explaining the event and the current office situation to the counselor, she thought it would be good for me to take some time off work. But I immediately responded, "What about my customers? What about my staff? They've been through so much already. I couldn't possibly think of leaving them right now!"

In a disturbing trend, the bank's needs had now become more important than my own personal well-being. I wouldn't take a leave of absence; I did, however, agree to follow her suggestion and have further consultation with a psychiatrist who specialized in work-related problems. At that appointment, the doctor listened intently as I described the recent series of events, asked a few questions, and then concurred with the counselor that I needed a break. I didn't like hearing that advice any better than the first time. Not only did I not want to abandon my staff, but Jeffrey and I desperately needed my paycheck. A leave was simply not a viable option, I thought.

Finally, I decided a therapist not associated with the bank would be able to give me an objective viewpoint and could make more appropriate suggestions on how to deal with the circumstances. I contacted noted San Francisco psychologist Dr. Brenda Wade, an African American sisterfriend whom I had known for several years and whose work I respected. After I related my banking experience to her, she looked at me in shock and said, "Glinda, those are horrendous conditions to be working under!" Ultimately she, too, suggested I take some time off—advice that I declined once again.

I knew, though, that the anxiety was catching up with me. I was overstressed trying to balance so many things at once—my husband's happiness, my job responsibilities, our creditors' requirements, employee problems, requests from my in-laws, even our dog's needs. I came to think that only I could fix things. I had assumed this weight gradually, over time. But now that these people expected me to handle it all, that made it worse. I became angry and resentful from giving, giving, giving. No one seemed to come to my rescue, and ultimately I turned the anger inward and became ashamed, embarrassed, and depressed. I was hardly eating or sleeping, and my weight dropped from 115 to 98 pounds.

The Holistic Road to Recovery

Three professionals hadn't been able to persuade me to take time off, not because they weren't skilled, but because of my extreme state of denial and dysfunction. But the morning I got on the scale and saw that I weighed less than 100 pounds, I saw my choices clearly. I knew that with another week in that environment, functioning at that pace, my health—in fact, my very life—would be at risk.

It was not worth my life, so I could see now that a leave of absence was truly necessary for me to regroup. It was a Wednesday morning when I went into the office, called my supervisor, and between sobs informed him that Friday would be my last day. Still, I hadn't anticipated the profound feelings of failure that came with taking this leave. Emotionally, I felt I had lost my sense of identity because I was no longer a bank manager. But during the leave of absence, I was able to do a major reevaluation of my life and my finances and begin a much-needed recovery. Ultimately, I decided that though banking had provided an excellent foundation, the time had come for me to move on. I resigned.

While on leave, my marriage had further deteriorated, but I made a pact with myself and Dr. Wade to commit to a conscientious effort for one year to save it. Jeffrey and I attended couples counseling briefly, and there we were introduced to new skills that enabled us to communicate with each other a little better. We tried talking together without accusing or blaming the other or becoming defensive.

Our couples counseling lasted only a short time, but Jeffrey and I continued to work on our relationship for the year I had committed to give it. By then it was evident that the common objectives, trust, and love we once shared had eroded and disappeared under the weight of our problems. Had we been able to communicate more effectively earlier, things might have turned out differently. But eventually, the time came for me to take definitive action, so I chose to move out of the house. Jeffrey and I were separated for about a month before I actually filed for divorce.

Because Jeffrey did not pay off any significant portion of our debt, creditors aggressively pursued me for payments. I was left with roughly $50,000 in consumer debt; our income property was in foreclosure; the house I had lived in was in default; I was on disability and I was going through a divorce—all at the same time.

It had always been my intention to be responsible for my obligations, but I knew that to be fair to myself, I had to explore all available options for relief. I contacted the Consumer Credit Counseling Service (CCCS), who advised me that my situation was so bad that I should just file bankruptcy. Two bankruptcy attorneys concurred with the CCCS. But an independent financial counselor gave me hope and explained how we could work together to put things right, using Debtors Anonymous meetings as an adjunct to our sessions. After thorough research, I decided that the individual financial counseling approach was the most appropriate solution for me because it was most in line with my beliefs and values.

It was an excruciatingly painful period. I almost never left the house unless I was going to therapy with Dr. Wade or to my financial counselor. I was so ashamed and embarrassed about what I had let happen. Family members and friends would call to check on me with apprehension and concern in their voices. But I thought, "Why don't they just leave me alone. It's too late now. Things are just too messed up." I even refused to open the curtains of my house to let sunlight in. For a while I kept my environment dark and dismal to match my state of mind.

Finally, a Breakthrough

Let's face it: Often we have to hit bottom, be broken down and humbled, before we're able to let go of old destructive beliefs and patterns and rebuild our lives on a healthy, solid foundation. For me, the breakthroughs didn't start to come until I was shocked by my life's circumstances and forced to come back down to earth from the fantasy world where I had lived for many years, seeing only what I wanted to see. Up until then, I was terribly self-righteous. I thought I knew all the answers. And I had to watch my world collapse around me before accepting the wake-up call. By then so much of my identity was tied up in job titles, a lush, materialistic lifestyle, and what other people thought about my situation that I lost my sense of who Glinda really was.

In private therapy, Dr. Wade helped me to see from my behavior that I had been "addicted" to Jeffrey. Extended periods of emotional distance between us made me crave any sign of his love, affection, and support. So I spent lots of money, hoping to gain his approval. During the latter part of our marriage when he showed occasional interest in or sensitivity toward me—or our problems—his attention could provide just enough of a "fix" to make me feel good for a little while. The "high" separated me from the reality of our wrecked lives. But when the high wore off, things would be no better than before.

I had subconsciously believed that if I were the main breadwinner (like Dad), my partner would be dependent on me (like Mom) and would never leave me. The truth of the matter is that dependent partners often abandon you emotionally if not physically. I realized I deserved to have more than that from my relationship. I'm worthy of a mate who is loving, affectionate, committed, and generous. I need not be too dependent or too independent. Being interdependent is a good balance.

I believe there are no accidents. When I was in the midst of my life crisis with career, marriage, and finances, I was forced to tap into my deepest inner reserves of energy to exercise my "gut muscles" and move my ego out of the way to seek help. God guided me to therapy, back to church, and to a 12-step support group called Co-Dependents Anonymous, where I learned I was not crazy for having these feelings and behaviors. Most important, I was not alone.

Early on my sister Yvonne said I had a lot of displaced anger. She was right. And eventually I was able to move beyond anger, hostility, and feeling like a victim. I was able to stop blaming others and acknowledge my role in my financial problems. I was also finally willing to accept that I had allowed everything that happened in my life and that there were no rewards for acting like a martyr. The more I was able to let go of the negative emotions and grieve the losses, the more clarity and confidence I was able to regain.

The Making of a Financial Recovery Specialist

Once I left a job and a marriage that no longer provided healthy environments for me, I began to embrace only business and personal relationships that were based on shared values and that nurtured my spirit. For years I continued a self-designed program that included counseling, support groups, and seminars on personal and financial healing. This "holistic" approach helped me understand the origins of my distorted beliefs and how they manifested themselves in my monetary habits. Prior to that, I had knowledge of the practical things that needed to be done to improve my financial situation—but over time it became clear that balancing my checkbook and making a budget was not enough. Unless my money mind-set was changed, I'd simply continue to create new and innovative ways to sabotage myself financially.

Once I regained stability after my financial and emotional crisis, I realized the value of my knowledge and experiences. I knew this was something I could teach to other people. That's when I founded Bridgforth Financial Management Group, a financial-counseling practice that specializes in a holistic approach to cash flow and debt management by integrating emotional and spiritual elements with practical techniques. I also bring to clients my personal experience, empathy, and a certain sensitivity that only someone who has lived with the shame of money dysfunction can understand.

Why This Book Is for Black Women

Now that you know my story, I hope that you will feel, "If she can make it through all that, achieve her goals, and find financial peace of mind, then maybe I can too!"

Originally I had planned to write a financial book geared to an audience of all ethnic backgrounds, because that has always been the makeup of my client base. But while writing my book proposal I noticed that the examples of clients I had chosen to illustrate the financial problems related to low self-esteem were almost all African American women. This is not to say that women of other cultures don't have self-esteem issues—they most certainly do. Everyone has these problems, but black women have more to contend with in developing a healthy sense of self in this society, and as a result, they often have a harder time establishing healthy financial habits. The range of resulting money problems can vary greatly, from anorexic-type patterns, where we avoid money or are afraid to spend it, to bulimic-type patterns of obsessive binge spending.

My financial program is distinctive because it doesn't focus exclusively on the hardware of personal finance. I don't advise, "Stop using your credit cards," and then exhort, "Just do it!" or "Just say NO!" Chances are you've already heard this message a million times before. Intellectually you know that it makes sense, but emotionally it somehow hasn't worked for you. A holistic financial program, however, helps you understand your attitudes and identify your behavior patterns. The techniques assist you in making the cultural, historical, emotional, and spiritual connections necessary to build a solid financial foundation for yourself and your family.

How to Use This Book

To begin financial healing, it's important to let go of negative energy by forgiving yourself and anyone else for whom you might harbor feelings of blame. Remember, my ex-husband and I had accumulated together $50,000 in debt that made me slow to forgive him and myself. But I did it eventually. When I paid off the last debt from that relationship, I felt a glorious sense of relief and accomplishment that restored my self-confidence. I keep it foremost in my mind, however, that compulsive debting is as addictive as compulsive drinking. To remain debt free, I must take it just one day at a time. With God's help and conscientious efforts to keep my money straight, I know I can do it.

I no longer have intense regrets about the financial chaos I created in my life because it gave me an opportunity not only to find my own way back, it also gave me my new and productive life as a financial recovery specialist with the expertise to help so many other people help themselves. I have a lot to be thankful for: I dearly love the work of helping people change their lives and find financial peace of mind.

Chapter One, the chapter you are reading now, is one of three chapters in Part One, "Preparing Your Mind for Financial Success." The next two chapters in this section focus on guiding you through your own internal psychological inventory about your relationship with money. This focusing will help you identify beliefs and emotions that sabotage your financial success, and uses exercises and tools like the genogram to analyze and evaluate money messages you have inherited from your family. I think of this internal work as the software of my program to get your money straight.

Part Two, "Seven Prescriptions for Financial Health and Healing," integrates the software with the hardware and provides a practical framework of basic money-management procedures—proven cash-management and debt-management tools and strategies that can enhance your economic future. If you commit yourself to the systems and exercises in this section of the book, you will be able to:

- Recognize and move through any counterproductive ideas you may have developed about money, focus on why you've held such views, and change your thinking for the better

- Become aware of exactly how much income you need to meet your basic needs and live comfortably

- Learn to use effectively the recommended tools and techniques for keeping track of your finances

- Pay off your debts, remain debt free, and make it a habit to save and invest money for your future

Part Three, "Beyond Getting It Straight," is the concluding section of the book. It points you toward inspirational examples of sisters who have gone the whole nine yards, finding financial peace of mind and increasing personal net worth beyond their dreams.

In the book, I'll be coaching you through a series of exercises that will help you master each piece of the financial healing program. I strongly recommend that you keep the papers on which you do these exercises so that you can look back on them periodically to chart your growth and progress. You might want to set aside a brightly colored folder marked *Girl, Get Your Money Straight!* and keep it on your home desk or worktable. Put a photograph of yourself in happy times on the cover—one with a big smile. You might even want to tuck the folder into your briefcase or keep it with you in the car or on the bus or subway so that in moments of weakness—when you're tempted to go out for an expensive lunch or stop off on the way home to buy a new outfit after a bad day—you'll be able to pull it out and tell yourself, "Honey, you've got better things to do with your money!" Besides, there's no better motivator than a glance back at how far you've already come.

There are three key things that I'd like you to keep in mind as you start off down the road to financial healing:

1. **Be accepting of yourself and your present circumstances:** Courageously examine your prior financial actions—or inaction—knowing you can move forward from where you are now only by making changes.

2. **Be grateful for life's lessons:** How often do you hear somebody say, "Thank God, this past-due electric bill has a twenty-four-hour notice to disconnect!" Probably never. Typically, we don't look at such crises as blessings. But if you do, you'll see that they can serve as timely wake-up calls to tighten up our game.

3. **Be patient with yourself:** Changing your habits from unconscious consumption to conscious wealth-building takes time. Measure your progress from month to month, using the strategies and suggestions in this book, and don't forget to give yourself mental and spiritual reinforcement—an important part of the holistic financial healing process.

Okay, girl, are you ready? Let's get your money straight!

Exercise One: Meet Your Money

In this exercise, I want you to have a heart-to-heart conversation with one of your most intimate companions: your money. Conduct a dialogue with it as if it were a person. Yes, that's right. Put your pen to paper and write it all down until you've said everything you can say.

You may want to do this in the form of a letter or maybe as entries in your private journal. Include your observations, feelings, concerns, issues, and fears about money. Write down every idea that comes to mind—positive or negative. Then, when you've said it all, ask your friend Money to reply. Write Money's answer and continue the conversation until you and Money have made peace.

How will you know when you've made peace? When you suddenly feel lighter, like a load only you knew you were carrying seems to have risen from your shoulders. It's easy enough to talk to ourselves and others about our money problems. What's more difficult is secretly admitting to ourselves what money really means to us, whether we see it as something that makes us feel important, a validation of our otherwise humdrum existence, a windfall to do with as we wish, or a responsibility for which we are accountable.

My client, Shauna, got a real kick out of doing this exercise. Here's what her conversation was like:

Dear Money: I thought you grew on trees. It's been a long, hard lesson to realize, but now I know you don't. Sometimes I treated you like water, thinking you were flowing from everywhere. Then I got this crazy, horrible feeling when you dried up. You know, that feeling of deprivation. Why, as important as you are, didn't they teach a class on you when I was in school? I could have learned to understand your influence at an early age, not in my mid-thirties. You are so powerful!

Dear Shauna: All I am is energy. You should use me like you use all energy. I'm just energy! I wish you could get the word out that I'm not good or evil. I'm not here to hurt you or cause you pain. I'm here to assist you. And I wish you wouldn't use me as an excuse to cover up other stuff or issues that are really bugging you. You know what I'm talking about.

SHAUNA: I *don't* know what you're talking about.

MONEY: Need I tell you? Your weight, your insecurities, your relationships, your daddy, your mama, white men in corporate America, food. Need I go on? Stop using me to solve your issues around these things.

SHAUNA: Wow! You really know how to hurt a girl! Oh, yeah, I know you said you weren't here to hurt me. Thanks for the advice. I'm going to try to improve my relationship with you. I'm going to love and appreciate you and stop taking you for granted. If I can do those things for you, Money, I can do them for myself. Thanks.

Chapter Two

A Closer Look at History

Tamika had always known how to make an entrance, and the afternoon of our monthly booklovers' meeting was no exception. Tamika honked as she drove past the group of us headed toward the entrance of the local hotel where we were meeting. Stopping her car, she waited for the uniformed parking attendant to open the door to her new silver Lexus. We all stopped dead in our tracks as this striking sister stepped from her car wearing a white-lace tailored ensemble and matching shoes, which she later explained she'd had custom made during a recent trip to Nigeria.

Tamika, thirty-two, a tall and statuesque divorcee, owns a fashionable beauty salon. Over the years, while serving as both mother and father to her now twelve-year-old daughter, she has worked hard.

Starting out with a one-stall shop in a run-down section of the city, she scrimped and saved until she could move her shop up to a busy downtown corner location, where she oversaw several stylists. Judging from her new car and clothes, business was indeed booming. She was living large, and she certainly deserved it.

After our group meeting, Tamika invited me for a spin in her new ride. But she startled me by candidly brushing aside my compliments on how well she appeared to be doing. "I always thought that if I made as much money as I do, I'd be set," she said. "But I'm spending it faster than it comes in. I took home $100,000 last year, but I owe about $63,000. I wake up at night in a panic about what I bought the day before.

"A couple of weeks ago, someone offered to buy my shop," she confided. "Girl, I was *so* tempted, but that place is my baby. Besides, soon as they put the money in my hands, God knows I'd just blow it and have nothing left." She paused as if exhausted from the weight of her words. "I haven't told anyone else. My mother earns as much in a year as I do in three months, but she owns a house and has saved money. She'd be so ashamed of me if she really knew of my situation."

Tamika then asked me to work with her as her financial counselor. I explained that I wasn't a bookkeeper or an accountant who would help her keep track of how much she had in the bank or scold her if she went off her budget. What I would help her do, I said, was develop a *Spending Plan* and show her how she could pay off her outstanding debts. But even that wouldn't be enough, I added; unless she was willing to *explore and transform the beliefs and attitudes* she had developed about money as a result of childhood events, family, and cultural messages, they would continue to drag her back into debt regardless of how much money she earned.

For the next several months, Tamika visited my office every two weeks as she worked at changing her relationship with money. In Tamika's first session, we assessed her monetary needs and clarified just how much she owed and to whom. Tamika actually owed a total of $66,000, or $3,000 more than she had initially estimated. She described herself as "scatterbrained" and chalked her staggering debt up to being a poor manager. She simply didn't see a connection between her money problems and how she felt about herself.

Getting to the Heart of the Matter

A few weeks later, Tamika arrived at my office for our scheduled session carrying a shopping bag. Looking somewhat ashamed, she announced, "I bought a St. John suit. I know it wasn't in my Spending Plan, and I'm gonna take it back." I reminded her that I was not there to judge her, and that the last thing she needed was to feel more shame. We spent the session reviewing her spending patterns over the last month, and she had actually done pretty well sticking to her plan, except for today's slip. So I suggested a homework assignment: I asked her to consider what she'd been feeling earlier today when she purchased her new $800 suit. Tamika was somewhat reluctant, but during our next appointment, I saw that something had shifted within her.

"When I went into the department store, I was there just to browse and didn't plan to buy anything," she began. "But after I went inside, I decided to go up to look at designer suits. This white saleswoman in that department kept ignoring me, just like I wasn't there, and lavished attention on another shopper, who was white. I know I should be used to this by now, but I was furious! There I was, dressed like somebody who would be shopping in a store like that, and that other customer looked like she'd wandered in off a farm. Next thing I knew I was trying on that St. John suit and whipping out my credit card. Deep down inside, I wanted to show that saleswoman I was somebody."

I congratulated her for recalling and recounting these feelings, but I encouraged her to keep digging, to consider the experience from the perspective of childhood incidents when she was made to feel that she wasn't good enough. Tamika mentioned her father's abandoning the family when she was very young and his never returning to see her. She recalled subsequent years of caring for her younger siblings while her mother worked two and sometimes three jobs to support the family. "I hate feeling insignificant, like I don't matter," she said. "The more financially successful you look, the more respect you get."

Tamika began looking back over many purchases and decisions that had been made on the basis of emotional needs rather than what she actually required for living comfortably. "At first I didn't believe you when you said my debts had something to do with how I secretly felt," she admitted. "I just wanted to get the numbers straight. But what happened to me as a kid or what happened last week with that saleswoman and my bills go hand in hand, don't they?"

We would work together several more months, but that day marked a breakthrough for Tamika. In addition to our bimonthly meetings, she engaged in the self-discovery and healing exercises included in this chapter and the ones that follow, tapping into the positive spiritual power that exists within all of us. Tamika transformed her life, thus rewriting for her daughter damaging family messages that caused her to fear she would never have enough. The day she paid off her last debt, twenty-four months after she first unburdened herself to me in that Sunday-afternoon ride in her Lexus, she was beaming. With her mind and spirit working in sync, she conveyed to the world that she was a woman of worth without having to display it through expensive clothes and accessories.

How Culture Influences Our Emotional Attitudes

At times even the best of us have contended with insecurities that make us feel that we are less than we are. Whether we are black, white, male, or female, when we are psychologically vulnerable, we may allow negative experiences encountered in daily life to whittle away our self-esteem, leaving us feeling ungrounded and out of sorts. In my experience, a diminished sense of self-worth frequently drives unhealthy behavior with money. As black women, our unique cultural history, family messages, and day-to-day life experiences contribute to a high level of self-criticism and self-doubt, which may ultimately play out in money mismanagement.

In their 1999 book *What Mama Couldn't Tell Us about Love: Healing the Emotional Legacy of Slavery, Celebrating Our Light,* psychologist Dr. Brenda Wade and her coauthor, journalist Brenda Lane Richardson, examine the legacy of the more painful aspects of African American history on our emotional conditioning, our capacity for self-love, and our intimate relationships. They assert that our people have "a legacy of feelings and beliefs that developed from our collective experiences, beginning with the kidnapping of our African ancestors when they were dragged in chains to the New World."

Dr. Wade and Mrs. Richardson go on to suggest that embedded in African American culture is a belief system that grew out of the disruption and losses of slavery and the violence and humiliation of life under Jim Crow laws, and continues to be reinforced by the subtler forms of today's racism. Their book vividly describes how these things have shaped what we believe about ourselves, our behavior on all levels, and what it takes to transform our thinking and behavior toward healthier models.

Most African Americans need go back only a few generations to identify ancestors who were sharecroppers. These men and women sold their labor to landowning planters for a share of the crops their labor produced. It may have sounded like a reasonable arrangement, but the way it typically worked was anything but fair: Our sharecropping predecessors were consistently taken advantage of, overcharged for supplies and rents by their landlords. Consequently, they became more indebted after each season even though they toiled day in and day out and often brought in good crops. Encouraged to buy on credit from plantation stores that systematically overcharged them, black sharecroppers usually only sunk deeper into entangling obligations.

Unfortunately, many black people today feel as powerless as their sharecropping forebears because they can't seem to get ahead despite hard work and even greater opportunities. Today we have more control over our lives and more options to choose from, but a strong sense of pessimism still lingers within our culture: that the world is a harsh and alien place and we can expect to get very little from it to sustain us. Such a perspective is passed from generation to generation through attitudes and messages like "A black person can never get ahead" or "I've got two strikes against me: I'm black and I'm female."

Our cynicism is certainly understandable given how we came to live in this country. But looking back at our history to appreciate the origins of these attitudes can also give us valuable perspective to free ourselves from them when they are no longer appropriate. More important, we should also appreciate that the courage and perseverance that our ancestors displayed in trying times is also a part of our own genetic makeup. We can view the heroic efforts of our forefathers and foremothers with pride and admiration, claim the gut muscles they used to survive the hardship of their times as our own, and exercise those muscles to improve our circumstances, financially and in every other way.

The Challenges of African American History and Heritage

The 1977 miniseries *Roots* had a profound impact on the country when it first aired. Over 130 million viewers made the adaptation of Alex Haley's Pulitzer Prize–winning book of the same name the highest-rated and most talked about program up to that time. The film had both blacks and whites glued to television sets for eight nights, reliving the Haley family's agonizing but ultimately triumphant odyssey from Africa to the New World. The miniseries dramatically revealed to the nation an aspect of black history that is still largely absent from textbooks even though it's an integral part of larger American history.

The truth is, this aspect of our history is excruciatingly difficult to look at whether you're black or white. People from all over the world—from Albania to Vietnam—have come to America seeking a better life, and many of these immigrants experienced bias and prejudice. But African Americans are the only people who came to this country against their will. Being stolen from Africa and brought here to be used as free labor was the beginning of a horrendous journey. But it was also the beginning of the saga of a people with a strong will and indomitable human spirit.

People of African descent, in fact, have a rich history to be proud of before we even came to the New World. Many early African civilizations enjoyed tremendous prosperity because of diverse practices in agriculture, industry, and commerce. Every African tribe had distinctive skills and knowledge on which they built economic well-being. Pygmies specialized in manufacturing bark cloth and fiber baskets; Ashantis wove rugs and carpets; Hottentots made clothing from textiles, skins, and furs; and Yoruba made ornamental objects from silver and gold. According to noted historian John Hope Franklin in his book *From Slavery to Freedom: A History of Negro Americans*, King Mansa-Musa, ruler of Mali, once financed a pilgrimage by using "eighty camels to bear his more than 24,000 pounds of gold." This kind of travel, frequently led by kings, did a great deal to stimulate trade and further develop African civilization and culture. So in fact we have a history of prosperity, commercial savvy, and financial ingenuity in our blood.

Our ancestors were enslaved in the sixteenth century to satisfy the European colonial need in the New World for laborers to clear the land and cultivate the fields. Estimates show that between the sixteenth and nineteenth centuries, almost 14 million men, women, and children were taken from Africa. During these hellish times, our foremothers were more than just passive victims of economic expansion. They played an integral, if too frequently unheralded, role in resistance and the struggle for freedom—many demonstrating genius, ingenuity, and extraordinary courage as they sought to establish and maintain a certain quality of life for themselves and their families.

After the Civil War, although newly freed blacks never received the infamously promised "40 acres and a mule" from abandoned and confiscated plantations in the South, our people maintained faith in God and in our own abilities to advance. We pursued education, and $5 million was spent by the government to found black colleges like Hampton, Morehouse, Fisk, and Howard University, which continue to be prestigious educational institutions and prime sources of leadership in the black community today. The nation's historically black colleges have graduated the vast majority of this nation's prominent black achievers in the twentieth century, including late billionaire Reginald Lewis, a modern-day captain of industry, and Earl Graves, founder of *Black Enterprise* magazine.

Previously accustomed to coping with hard times and subsistence living, some blacks didn't experience the same plunge in living standards during the Great Depression as more financially stable whites. Before World War II, most blacks lived on farms, grew their own food, and were basically self-sufficient. The increasing number of blacks who lived in the cities, however, were more vulnerable economically because many of the unskilled jobs they had traditionally held were reclaimed by unemployed whites; hence the saying "Last hired, first fired." Many urban African Americans who held jobs, whether in domestic service or the factories, were laid off, and these job losses sent ripples through the economy of the black community, since unemployed black workers didn't have the same kind of money to support the service businesses in their own communities that relied on their patronage, such as grocery stores, beauty shops, funeral homes, and doctor and dentist offices.

Because of discriminatory job markets and lower wages, black people since Emancipation have always had to work twice as hard— usually holding down two or three jobs just to survive and support their families. Though the overt discrimination supported by law prior to the Civil Rights movement is remote from the daily experience of today's youth, we need only imagine how overwhelming it must have seemed sometimes for our forebears in this land of prosperity. They were restricted by a whole body of laws in their efforts to forge ahead. The human attitudes of despair and resignation coexisted with the prevailing daily heroism of covert and overt resistance, yet it created a legacy of self-esteem issues that each generation had to confront.

It's natural to ask "Why have our people had to suffer so many injustices?" But it's more important to acknowledge how our ancestors' endurance has created opportunities for us to experience lives without bondage—including life without modern *financial* bondage. The discrimination that still intrudes in the day-to-day life of twenty-first-century black women can be subtle, obscure, and often undercover, but it still can be very debilitating. Sometimes we get demoralized and don't have the energy to respond directly to every racial affront or slight in order to have our grievances addressed promptly. We, like other Americans, are often easily seduced by a consumer culture that links our status in life to what we own. But we must be especially wary of acting out financially—of consuming more than we should just to soothe ourselves after an incident that diminishes the sense of basic equality and respect that white people take for granted.

Yes, our responses to our own cultural history can be an underlying cause of how and why we use and misuse money today. Yes, although there have been great strides made by our people over the last 350 years, some individuals of other cultures continue to treat us unfairly. Unfortunately, life is not always fair. But we can use this information to help us connect the dots, draw conclusions, and keep our eyes focused on creating a quality of life that is financially balanced and spiritually fulfilling. If we learn to model the courage and tenacity of our ancestors, whose traits are a part of our very being and substance, we can persevere through today's challenges with our self-esteem intact and our finances in control.

Contemporary Workplace Woes

Asha, age twenty-six, was a beautiful, dark chocolate-brown sister with a radiant smile and an effervescent personality. At five feet eight inches tall and 175 pounds, she was a big woman, perhaps even overweight by mainstream standards. But her husband, a man of six feet four inches and 225 pounds, adored her and often affirmed how he and many other brothers "liked a woman with some meat on her bones." Married for five years, she and her spouse hadn't been blessed with children, so they focused their attention on each other, their jobs, and their San Jose community, where they owned a large three-bedroom home.

Asha's positive mental attitude and shining inner light easily attracted people to her. She was intelligent, enthusiastic, and ambitious. Determined to better herself as a young woman, Asha had worked a full-time job as a receptionist while taking college courses at night for six years before earning her undergraduate degree in finance. She spent the next two years working successfully as a sales representative for a mortgage broker before seeing a classified ad from a major bank that was seeking a business development officer. Her interest was piqued. She forwarded her résumé and after a series of interviews was hired.

If that sounds like a simple tale of upward mobility, it isn't: Asha is, in fact, the sister I mentioned briefly in Chapter One, the woman my supervisor suggested I pay a lower salary than the blue-eyed, blond-haired candidate with no experience. I never discussed with Asha what it took to get her hired at what I considered a fair and just salary at the bank. But chances are that since then, she's had to face other subtle discriminations within the company.

The same subtext underlay the highly publicized 1994 class action suit against Texaco, Inc. The complaint alleged the company had failed to promote black employees to upper-level jobs and had fostered a racially hostile environment. During the two-year investigation of the case, secret tape recordings of Texaco executives were discovered that revealed black employees being referred to as (the N word) and "black jelly beans." In addition, the executives discussed destroying and withholding documentation pertinent to the case.

After the tapes were released in 1996, there was public outrage and denunciation followed by a national boycott of Texaco products. Chairman Peter Bijur apologized publicly to the African American employees for the comments and behavior of the company's executives. He ordered a settlement of the case that resulted in a $176-million award, the largest in the history of employment race discrimination litigation.

If you think the Texaco suit is not only an extreme example but maybe even yesterday's news—such blatant workplace discrimination couldn't possibly carry over into the twenty-first century—the federal suit by eight black current and former employees of Coca-Cola, who accuse the multinational corporation of denying blacks fair pay, promotions, raises, and performance reviews, is unfortunate evidence to the contrary. Former Coca-Cola human resources manager Larry Jones has alleged that at Coca-Cola, black employees earn $27,000 to $32,000 a year less than whites in the same positions.

While Coca-Cola denies these allegations of discrimination, supporters of the plaintiffs took their case to the company's annual meeting in 2000 and are moving to organize a national boycott.

The disparaging comments and insensitive racial attitudes caught on tape at Texaco are just an example of what is still prevalent in society and corporate culture. Sometimes it's blatant racial epithets, and sometimes it's a condescending demeanor toward people of color, and almost everyone can point to pay differentials that many feel are the result of discrimination. Regardless, black women feel and know when we're being patronized or viewed as inadequate. Usually we just shrug these incidents off and keep quiet because they happen so frequently in our day-to-day experiences, but they do affect us economically and limit our ability to break through the glass ceiling that too often blocks us from reaching upper management.

It is often these types of challenges—both inside and outside the workplace—that attack our self-esteem and make us prone to spend excessive amounts of money in an effort to seek respect from whites and to make ourselves feel better. We may subconsciously be rebelling against the very financial constraints placed upon us by less-than-equal-opportunity employers. In reality, the buying fix provides only short-term emotional relief and leaves a long-term financial detriment especially when we spend money that was allocated for other expenses or create debt that will take years to pay off.

Public Accommodations: The Restaurant Blues

Both because of hectic schedules and increased spending power, our generation more than any previous one has adopted a lifestyle that makes eating out as much the norm as cooking meals at home. Restaurants are more than just places to nourish ourselves—they are a major part of our recreational and social interaction.

My sister, Ann, loves to eat in fine establishments. She once described telephoning an upscale eatery in Los Angeles to make dinner reservations and was told about the dress code—no jeans or tennis shoes allowed. She and her guest complied, of course, but while enjoying their expensive meal noticed several white patrons dining while dressed in jeans and tennis shoes. Ann felt insulted and offended by the selective preference given to the other customers.

Naturally she wondered: Does the restaurant apprise all individuals who make telephone reservations of the dress code, or was she informed because she sounded black? Would she and her party have been turned away at the door if they were inappropriately dressed? Was the restaurant somehow especially concerned that black folks would arrive at a nice restaurant underdressed? Many African Americans experience similar situations on a daily basis—is it any wonder we feel the need to spend so much money on our exterior image when we're so often viewed as unacceptable?

Unfortunately, the dress code is not the only issue we have to deal with in restaurants. The success of the 1956 Montgomery bus boycott enabled us to sit anywhere we choose on buses. But, over forty years later, society hasn't completely gotten the message about our equal rights. For example, one day I suggested to an African American male friend that we have lunch at a particular restaurant that served great food. I had previously had a fabulous meal there with a white colleague and was excited about turning my friend on to a new place to eat. I was craving the incredible seafood linguine and could almost smell the wonderful garlic aroma as we made the twenty-minute drive to a predominantly white suburb outside Oakland.

Upon arriving and requesting a table for two, the hostess smiled, walked us toward the back of the restaurant, and offered us seats. My date looked around the room and, spotting another vacant table that seemed a better choice, asked for that one instead. The hostess then quite pleasantly seated us at a table near the front window. After she stepped away, my friend looked at me, winked, and said, "You have to ask for what you want because they don't want us out here anyway." He then went on to comment on how frequently blacks are seated in the rear of the restaurants. And sure enough, for the next hour and a half we watched almost every black patron who entered be directed to a table located in the rear of the room.

I learned a great lesson that day. Granted, many restaurants do not follow this discriminatory practice, but in the past I had never been aware enough to look for it either. Today, I try not to be paranoid. I am, however, suspicious whenever seated "in the booth, in the back, in the corner, in the dark"—especially if I'm not on a romantic date. I'm conscious of instances when I feel pushed to the back, hidden out of sight from white patrons, and made to feel unworthy, as if society is telling me "You don't belong here."

African Americans often take a deep breath and let this kind of affront pass without comment. But, in fact, with our feelings hurt and our dignity diminished, we may unconsciously grope for ways to build up our self-esteem. We may find ourselves ordering a more expensive meal from the menu and/or leaving excessively large tips to prove that we can afford to be there. Of course, doing this is not a problem if you can afford it and if you are simply ordering the meal you came there to eat. I love a good lobster as much as the next person, but if I order it solely because it will increase my esteem in the eyes of a waiter or waitress, that's not only a waste, it's counterproductive. Emotionally, I give my power away and end up rewarding others for bad behavior. More important, it's unwise financially and will not help me get or keep my money straight.

Shopping While Black

The mixed cues we typically experience as a lack of respect for us as black people don't surface just in the workplace and in restaurants. There's also the "shopping while black" phenomenon—where brothers are followed around in retail stores as if each one is a potential shoplifter; or where sisters are ignored by salesclerks in upscale stores as if we hadn't the means to buy anything. I've heard that Oprah Winfrey spoke about how she once had trouble gaining access to an exclusive retail store. Imagine that—one of the most popular media personalities in the country and the fourth-wealthiest entertainer in the United States, according to a 1998 *Forbes* magazine article, disrespected by employees of a retail store because of her race! If Oprah can be so rudely "dissed," what chance does the average black woman have?

At least Oprah was in the position to use her nationally syndicated television show to express her frustration, humiliation, and anger, vowing before an audience of millions never to set foot in that store again.

But few of us everyday black women receive the same kind of hearing and satisfaction after such a run-in. Last year a friend gave me a gift certificate to a well-known spa. I had heard fabulous things about the place and was excited about partaking in its pampering and rejuvenation. Unfortunately the experience turned out to be less enjoyable than I anticipated because an unpleasant tone was set from the start. After being led to a dressing room and instructed to remove my clothing, I was taken aback when the attendant handed me a terry-cloth bathrobe that was ratty and threadbare. Too dumbfounded to ask for another robe, I thought, "Gee, this place isn't as plush as I expected, but maybe this is the best robe they have."

As I sat waiting for my facial, there was another woman in the lounge with me. I noticed that her robe looked fine, but I tried to put it out of my mind because I didn't want to create a scene. My shabby robe was just a coincidence, the luck of the draw, and not racially motivated, I reasoned. Then one by one, as the next six women entered, all Caucasian, I noticed that no one had a robe as old as mine, no threads unraveling from their collars or sleeves. That's when I got pissed.

I mulled over this situation throughout the spa treatment and thus didn't fully enjoy it in my far-from-relaxed state. In the end, as a recourse, I chose not to tip the attendant who gave me the bathrobe. But I also decided not to say anything to her or to management because I felt the need to process my feelings and determine if I was being overly sensitive. Furthermore, I knew that I was physically in a danger zone—namely, in close proximity to a group of department stores. It would have been far too easy to do some "retail therapy" to ease the uncomfortable feelings I was experiencing.

I relate this personal story to show how even the most professionally self-assured woman can have her self-confidence shaken. Emotionally stressful circumstances make us question our self-worth. Seeking an immediate means to feeling better might mean purchasing some new cosmetics or a new pair of Ferragamo shoes. In my case, neither of those items was on my shopping list for the day, so it became critically important for me to derail these urges and negative emotions through self-affirmation. About one minute of silently repeating the mantras "I am more than enough" and "I love and approve of myself every day in every way" helped me get past the stores without making any unplanned purchases. Later I explained what happened to two sisterfriends who had previously visited the spa, and neither had had a similar experience. So I chalked it up to being an isolated incident. But it remained in my memory bank as an example of how discrimination can quickly unravel our self-esteem and leave us vulnerable to poor monetary decisions.

I've always been an optimist at heart, looking at the world through rose-colored glasses. I grew up hearing my mom say, "If you go out looking for trouble, you'll surely find it." And that's a message I still believe. I also believe in the scriptural message "You reap what you sow" and I practice the Golden Rule, "Do unto others as you would have them do unto you." However, I believe that we should be not only conscious of what we say and do, but aware of what we feel.

In other words, the energy and vibrations we send out into the universe are the energy and vibrations we'll get back. So, sisters, don't go out into the world expecting negative things to happen or looking for discrimination. Rather, expect to be affirmed and received warmly everywhere you go and with everything you do. With this positive approach toward the world, you'll be in a better psychological position to demand appropriate redress when you don't receive the respect you deserve. You are here on the planet to identify and fulfill your purpose and should view everything you are as an asset to the world—you are a child of God, a spiritual being, and an African American woman.

The Distorted Mirror of the American Media

Whether the source is television, radio, magazines, newspapers, film, or the Internet, the media has an overwhelming impact on society and can be used powerfully to disseminate positive or negative messages about different cultures and groups of people. African Americans are no exception. A new study commissioned by People for Better Television indicates that sixty-two percent of African Americans feel that television entertainment does not represent them accurately. Kweisi Mfume, president and CEO of the National Association for the Advancement of Colored People (NAACP), called the lack of diversity in the 1999 fall season prime-time lineup "an outrage and a shameful display by network executives." The omission of minorities in leading roles in the twenty-six new shows that debuted means that sisters like us are systematically deprived of an opportunity to see ourselves as either working-class or professional individuals with the capacity to take care of our families, hold down jobs, pay our bills, and build satisfying careers.

George Fraser, author of the best-selling books *Success Runs in Our Race* and *Race For Success,* observes: "It's unfortunate that there are two dominant images of blacks in America. One is a negative image of welfare, crime, and drugs. That's all we see in the mainstream media today. And the other is a stereotypical positive image that we can sing and dance, play football, baseball, and basketball. When in fact the statistics don't bear out either one of those images." When you think of black people, which of those two images come to mind first? If you're like many Americans, it's probably the negative one. Television news and films have conditioned us to see blacks as gang-bangers, thieves, rapists, and prostitutes. Fraser goes on to say, "There are less than 10,000 black folks in America earning $100,000 a year (or more) by singing, dancing, playing football, baseball, and basketball. And less than 6 percent of our population is involved in drugs, or the criminal justice system in any way. That means less than 6 percent of our population is driving the image of 35 million people. What's wrong with that picture?"

Obviously, what's wrong is that the media projects an inaccurate and unjust view of who we are as a people. The two predominant images Fraser highlights represent a relatively few black people at extreme ends of the spectrum, leaving out the majority of our population who are hardworking citizens making significant contributions. Were it not for national black-owned magazines like *Ebony, Jet, Essence, Black Enterprise,* and *Emerge,* black-owned networks like BET, and hundreds of local weekly black newspapers and radio stations, we'd hardly know about the hundreds of thousands of ordinary African

Americans who are doing extraordinary things, because so infrequently do we see them profiled in the mainstream media. That's one of the reasons the popular annual *Essence Awards* program, broadcast in recent years on the Fox TV network, not only presents a great evening of black entertainment and celebrity watching but also acknowledges and celebrates a selection of everyday African Americans who are unselfishly making a major difference in their communities.

Picking up a long tradition of self-help that flourished before the Civil Rights Movement, Maria Denise Dowd, founder and executive producer of African American Women on Tour (AAWOT), the nation's foremost black women's empowerment conference, has created an environment for learning, healing, networking, rejuvenation, and transformation for thousands of sisters since 1991. She says: "The bottom line is, blacks still have to make a way—politically, socially, and economically—with or without government intervention. That's the role AAWOT plays. The conference educates and heavily promotes taking ownership of our destinies, homes, neighborhoods, careers, wealth, businesses, our children's education, and so on."

For many years AAWOT has inspired and motivated thousands of sisters around the country with the camaraderie, bonding, and love at AAWOT conferences. When African Americans are made aware of the phenomenal work of sisters like Maria Denise Dowd, our spirits are lifted, our hearts warmed, we feel better about each other as a people, and we feel better about ourselves.

How do you view your life today? Do you feel more or less enriched than you did a year ago? Do you feel a sense of prosperity and abundance? Are you optimistic about the future? The June 7, 1999, issue of *Newsweek* magazine devoted thirteen pages to this subject. The article "The Good News About Black America," written by Ellis Cose, contained insights and quotes from leaders with differing opinions, but it generally indicated a strong resurgence of black self-confidence and self-determination. Those blacks polled by *Newsweek* credited black churches (46 percent) and black self-help organizations (41 percent) for the upturn in black conditions.

Cose cited numerous examples and statistics on why this is the best time ever to be black in America. For instance, black income is at its highest level (median income for a family of four reached a record high of $34,644 in 1997); black unemployment at 8.9 percent is lower than it has been in a quarter of a century; with better medical care blacks are living longer and having healthier children; and finally, white kids and adults now choose African Americans as their heroes. Even the predominantly white 1999 champion U.S. women's soccer team named Jackie Joyner-Kersee, the African American Olympic gold medalist in track and field, as their role model.

Yes, improvement has been made in many areas, but we can't celebrate too much and risk becoming complacent because there are still major gaps between blacks and whites, even regarding the positive statistics mentioned above. Although it reached a new high, black median income was still $21,378 less than the average for whites; black unemployment remains more than twice the rate for whites, which is only 3.9 percent; the number of blacks admitted to state schools had a huge drop when California, Texas, and Washington eliminated affirmative action; the suicide rate among young black men has risen sharply; and the number of black men in prison is as high as ever.

Stereotypical images of African Americans presented in the media affect the way people perceive us and the way we perceive ourselves. As a people, these images make us feel like we contribute negatively to society or, even worse, have nothing to contribute at all. We're insignificant, not important, or totally ignored, as if we don't exist. We don't earn as much as whites and are compelled to spend more to make ourselves feel that we measure up. Many of us have little discipline to save and have a pattern of scrambling around in the days prior to each paycheck. We know it's a vicious cycle, yet we convince ourselves we have no choice. It's become a way of surviving emotionally.

Even though today's news still includes an inordinate amount of crime perpetrated by blacks and to a lesser extent the incidence of brutally and bigotry against blacks, the *Newsweek* survey shows we're making progress and African Americans are feeling better about the future. We still know there's a long way to go before the dream of Dr. Martin Luther King, Jr., is realized. Cose states: "Blacks remain, in substantial measure, a race apart in America: a race admired, even emulated, yet held at arm's length. It reflects a particular American schizophrenia. We embrace equality and yet struggle with it in reality. We have come so far, and yet we have not escaped the past."

Salving Our Wounds—With Money

The way black women behave with money is often a direct reflection of how we feel about ourselves. Granted, it's not just black women who have suffered losses that eventually affect their spending habits. But because we live in a society in which blacks are often both consciously and unconsciously made to feel rejected and unwanted, our childhood injuries are exacerbated. In other words, we keep getting rewounded.

Dr. Nancy Boyd-Franklin, psychologist and author of *Black Families in Therapy,* has written: "It is difficult to convey fully to someone who has not experienced [it] the insidious, pervasive, and constant impact that racism and discrimination have on the lives of Black people in America today. Both affect a Black person from birth until death and have an impact on every aspect of family life, from child-rearing practices, courtship, and marriage, to male-female roles, self-esteem, and cultural and racial identification. They also influence the way in which Black people relate to each other and to the outside world."

Racist incidents are so much a part of our daily lives that a lot of us simply shrug them off and keep going. But our subconscious takes note and clicks into our internalized neon sign that flashes hurtful messages such as "You're not good enough," "You're inadequate," "You'll never be loved," and "You'll never be accepted." So regardless of gender, age, education, intelligence, or income, these messages create low self-esteem and can cause us to feel insecure, uncomfortable, and incompetent with money management.

When our self-esteem is low, we often look outside ourselves to bolster weak egos. Some people turn to alcohol and drugs to enhance their sense of self. Some people overeat, become religious fanatics, and/or become sexually obsessed to numb the feelings of inadequacy.

But many of us—especially women—overspend. We overspend to fill emotional voids, to buy love, and to fend off feelings of rejection, anger, and depression. We think "retail therapy"—buying that BMW, Donna Karan suit, or Coach handbag—will make us feel better. And it temporarily does. But often before we arrive home, buyer's remorse has set in. We regret having made the purchases and ask ourselves "Why did I do that? Why did I spend so much money on something that I really don't need?" We begin to panic as we think "How will I ever cover the check I just wrote?" or "How can I possibly add another payment to an already overburdened budget?" We realize our destructive indulgence has once again created excruciating financial fear and given us a reason for self-loathing. Here are some of the common self-esteem-based pitfalls that black women succumb to all too often.

Looking for Love—In All the Wrong Places

Many complex socioeconomic patterns and psychosexual dynamics contribute to African Americans' current status as the ethnic group in the United States with the lowest marriage rates. That's another book entirely. But for the purpose of gaining an understanding of what fuels our own financial patterns and choices, it's important to note that the absence of a love relationship is a very common excuse sisters use to justify impulsive spending. If we feel there's not enough love, affection, recognition, appreciation, or attention in our personal lives, this triggers sadness, loneliness, and depression. These emotions create a feeling of scarcity and lack—and we try to fill the void however we can. All too often, we empty our wallets and expand our credit-card debt while trying to fill the hole in our hearts. Trust me, I speak from experience.

One afternoon several years ago, I was hanging out with my two best girlfriends, enjoying one another's company, having lunch, chatting about art, music, and fashion. Then without warning the conversation shifted to a dreaded subject: men.

As a recently divorced woman at that point in my life, I could have contributed some zingers to a male-bashing session. But these two women were not unhappy; rather, they were in "ideal" relationships. Their partners adored them and were devoted, honest, generous, loving, and committed. These women lived in beautiful homes, frequented the best restaurants, and vacationed in exotic places around the world.

On the other hand, I had not been in a relationship for a while. During that time, I found myself hosting my own private pity parties. My negative self-talk came from a victim consciousness. "I don't have anybody in my life," I moaned to myself. "Nobody loves me. Everybody else has somebody to love. Why don't I? What's wrong with me?"

Spending that afternoon with my girlfriends later spiraled into an evening of overwhelming anger. I couldn't understand why I wasn't able to get this part of my life together. I considered myself attractive, intelligent, and independent. In other words, a good catch! What more could a brother want?

Shortly after that frustrating evening, I happened to join a prosperity group through my church where the goal was to change our consciousness and attract more prosperity into our lives. Our homework was to spend fifteen minutes each night for thirty days meditating on a given set of positive affirmations.

One evening I settled into bed for the nightly ritual and began by reading the following meditation:

All my needs and desires are completely fulfilled by the I AM Presence of God, Pure Unconditioned Being. With my clear thinking I create the mental molds I desire for Spirit to fill full. Therefore I expect the enrichment of Love, Joy, Creativity, Money, and Supply in my experience, and I receive them.

I lay back with my eyes closed and contemplated the mental mold that I wanted to fill. Immediately the relationship void came to mind. I then began to visualize filling the void with not just a healthy, happy relationship but with a true "soul mate," a "king" who would treat me like a "queen."

After enjoying this vision for a few moments, I then asked myself, "Okay, who are the men that have been in my life in the last twelve months?" To my surprise, especially since I had felt there was so much lack in this area, my list totaled eleven men! These were people with whom I had shared a meal, enjoyed a movie, or dated over the past year. I asked myself, "Even though there were no love connections with these men, what was the 'gift' or 'value' that each one brought to my life?" Before I had made my way through half the list, I became overwhelmed with joy at the realization of abundance and prosperity that I had unknowingly been experiencing.

Some of the wonderful gifts I had received from these men were as follows:

- *Friend 1*: A longtime pal with a great heart. He had tremendous business acumen and we shared many stimulating intellectual and philosophical conversations. He was supportive and encouraging regarding my growing business as well as in helping me find a passion for something other than just my work.

- *Friend 2*: A devoted single parent who demonstrated such love and patience with his children that it made me, the quintessential career woman, receptive to having a family of my own

- *Friend 3*: A successful businessman who loved to wine and dine me

- *Friend 4*: He brought out the "kid" in me. Even though both of us were forty-something, we'd revert to acting like twelve-year-olds whenever we got together. There was lots of laughter and silliness. He was also affectionate and attentive.

- *Friend 5*: He was available! Not in a relationship or otherwise involved with anyone. He was very social, very consistent, and very proactive in planning dates.

This exercise proved to be one of the most profound experiences of my life. It demonstrated to me that by adapting an "attitude of gratitude" for all my experiences, I could recognize the value in each one.

I now know that there is abundance in the universe and that there is always enough when I count my blessings.

Previously, without this exercise, those prior feelings of lack and insecurity would have led me to a very dangerous place—to my clothes closet to evaluate my wardrobe! My pattern would have been to scrutinize every item on the rack and, of course, nothing would be satisfactory. Everything would be old, outdated, too long, too short, the wrong color, the wrong style, couldn't be coordinated with any other item, or had no shoes to match. I would have thought, "I have absolutely nothing to wear. If only I had the 'right' clothes, then I would be okay. I would be worthy, and, naturally, I would have a man in my life!" My final thought would of been "Nothing fits my body anyway because my body is not good enough!" I could have impulsively done tremendous financial damage at the shopping mall trying to change my external image, when it was my internal void of self-esteem and self-appreciation that needed attention.

"Keeping" Our Men—In More Ways Than One

In our eagerness to "catch" a man, we are sometimes willing to play "finders keepers." Many black women with low self-esteem think that in order to keep a man in today's society you must do more for him than other women. Consequently, we become more competitive for the affection of those with acceptable criteria and end up supporting them lock, stock, and barrel. We must be careful not to create chaos in our lives by assuming full financial responsibility and providing a carte blanche lifestyle for perfectly healthy and able-bodied brothers. It's a financial trap that too many sisters fall into.

As black women, we must choose to go it alone rather than buy the affections of a man. This can be a tough choice to make. I know of a woman who won a fellowship that required relocating from Oakland to Washington, D.C. According to the myth she'd heard, she would find ten black women for every black man in the nation's capital. However, as a recent divorcée with two small children, getting involved was the last thing on her mind, and she knew that this was an important step for her to make, careerwise. She did meet some brothers, but most wanted her to spend time with them without the children in tow. She didn't mind going out occasionally without the kids, but constantly juggling children and dates—and paying baby-sitters for the privilege—was no fun for either her or her wallet. Then a sisterfriend introduced her to a wonderful man who was also a single parent. From the beginning, all their children were included, which lessened the strain on her wallet. She was no longer making irresponsible financial choices just for the sake of having a man in her life. She and her man recently celebrated their twenty-second wedding anniversary. Her motto is a good one to embrace: "A man should simplify your life, not complicate it." This applies financially as well as romantically!

I May Be Broke, but I Look Good!

There are few things in life we can count on: death, taxes, and black folks dressed to the nines. African Americans have to "fall out" at the party just so, and be driving a luxury car to boot. And they will spend whatever it takes to look as good as, if not better than, everyone else.

We are classic American consumers who spend a great deal of money on external "stuff." In 1997, according to *Target Market News*, a leading authority on the black consumer market, blacks earned $392 billion in income. From these earnings, black households spent $21 billion on new and used cars and trucks, $25.2 billion on apparel products and services, $8.1 billion on home furnishings and equipment, and $7.4 billion on personal care products and services (up from $4.4 billion the previous year).

Black women in particular are very image conscious and feel they must look good in addition to showing visible signs of success. My own unscientific study indicates that regular weekly clients at black beauty salons spend on average, in addition to an exorbitant number of hours, $225 per month on hair care. This amount does not include any monthly spending on nails, facials, or massages, which more and more black women are viewing as necessities rather than luxuries.

For a date, party, concert, or other outing, we sisters must have a new outfit to wear. Vacations, holidays, professional meetings, personal empowerment conferences, and sorority, club, or church events have an expectation of serious shopping attached. For example, my client Kendra generally refuses invitations to African American–sponsored cruises because for her, going will mean watching folks stylin' and profilin'. "When I take a cruise, it's for relaxation, to be attended to and pampered," she says. "But when traveling with my people, there's too much pressure to purchase a new 'cruise' wardrobe. I feel compelled to spend because I don't want to be left out or on the edge."

Recently, while planning a cruise to celebrate a hard-earned job promotion, Kendra felt a strong urge to buy new formal dresses for the captain's night dinner parties. But when I encouraged her to honestly look at her current wardrobe, Kendra was able to find an elegant evening gown that she had worn only once and another dress that fit the occasion perfectly. Not only did she save money, she had money left over after the cruise because she examined her motives for spending money while on the trip! Kendra's cruise photographs were fabulous, proof positive of a statement I heard from Dr. Bertice Berry, author, speaker, and former talk show host, who says, "Wearing that outfit for a second time . . . means you just look good twice!"

It's the same for holiday spending and gift giving. In order to feel a part of the family, we buy out of expectation or obligation. There's nothing wrong with taking care of ourselves or being generous to others if we can afford it and if it's self-motivated. But problems arise when we do it because of external reasons or if we're creating debt in the process.

So where do these urges come from? Why do black women continue this pattern at any price? One reason is that as children we rarely got clothes unless it was a special event. If jackets or shoes wore thin, or were damaged, torn, or lost, we just had to "make do" until the next special event.

Psychologist Dr. Brenda Wade agrees that's part of it but feels there's a more significant reason at the core. "It's shame. Black women feel they are not good enough and must compensate in some way. It's noise in the background that's always there related to our self-esteem and self-worth." She adds, "That new outfit provides a temporary confidence boost, but the deeper issues still need to be explored." Our issues with self-esteem, image, and people pleasing have made our lives painfully complex by making perception and perfectionism imperative—even if that means using cash advances to live on. We frantically try to prove we are as good as or better than everyone else and thrive on being acknowledged by others for our visual signs of success—especially with our clothes, because we love to receive compliments. This is the case for many of us who, even though personable and talented in our own right, are devastatingly broke yet have to make sure we look good regardless of the financial turmoil it causes.

Sunday-Go-to-Meeting

Churches have long been a center of influence in the black community. An estimated 80 percent of African Americans attend religious services regularly, versus 62 percent of the general population. Religious faith was largely responsible for our ancestors' ability to sustain themselves through the many atrocities of our cultural history. But even here money plays an interesting role. In Oakland, for example, 175 of the largest black churches deposit an estimated $780 million a year in one Bay Area bank alone. The same is true in other cities and states with significant black populations. According to *Target Market News,* African American households contributed $4.1 billion nationwide to churches and religious institutions in 1996. Some black churches collect substantial amounts of money and have generously financed black banks, credit unions, insurance companies, and residential facilities.

However, religious participation is also a major source of cultural pressure and financial expectation for black people. Image competition starts in the traditional black church when mothers work very hard each Sunday to make sure their children look perfect, like little models. Kids are threatened with beatings if they play, get dirty, or mess up their clothes or hair before arriving at church. Black folks show up for church, and everybody tries to outdo everybody else, from the elaborate Sunday hats to the decked-out Easter ensembles.

In addition to the expense associated with looking good for church, there are usually three or four collections taken per Sunday. Ministers coerce congregants to give to the general fund, the building fund, the missionary fund, the pastor's anniversary, and so on, as the choir sings, "The more you give, the more He gives to you." Dropping large bills into the collection plate has long been a source of power and prestige. And often because blacks have no other means to power and prestige in society, they use the black church to fulfill this need. In addition, many black women are generally inclined to tithe 10 percent of their salary to the church regardless of the strain it may put on their finances. One client was past due on her credit-card payments and $114,000 in debt, which included student loans and an outstanding balance on a luxury car. She remained adamant about tithing because it was "her way to get into heaven."

Granted, most ministers give much of themselves to their congregants and are constantly pulled in different directions. And they deserve a comfortable lifestyle to rest and rejuvenate their spirit in order to provide religious support for the community. But if your minister lives in a luxury home, drives a Cadillac, and insists on your tithing 10 percent of your income while you are consistently behind on your rent and unable to meet your monthly bills, something is wrong with that picture. You should rethink your priorities and adjust your contributions until you are on more solid financial ground.

Another aspect to be conscious of when tithing 10 percent is the belief that "as long as I tithe my 10 percent, God will take care of everything else." There is great danger in failing to accept personal responsibility. You must do a reality check and make sure that every two or three months or so you're not seeking a bailout or rescue from family and friends in order to pay your rent, car loan, or other expenses through the month. This is not being financially responsible or a good steward of the resources God provides for you.

Begin Your Healing: Affirmations As Healing Tools

Our ancestors and parents couldn't teach what they didn't know, so we can't blame our cultural upbringing for all our financial difficulties. But now that you've started to assess your money mind-set, you can plan to pass on healthy messages to our future generations. To attain and sustain financial health, a positive frame of reference about yourself and life in general is crucial. Affirmations—directed positive declarations—can aid in combating the negative programming we absorb, by replacing it with an abundance mentality and optimistic expectations. They help release the ties that bind us to unhealthy beliefs and destructive financial patterns. They also alter the deep-seated belief systems and attitudes that act as barriers to financial success.

Three guidelines to keep in mind when framing effective affirmations are (1) The affirmation must be stated as if it has already been accomplished for a more powerful and energetic effect. For example: *I am a money magnet.* Not: *I will become a money magnet.* (2) The goal or objective must be reasonable. It's okay to choose things that are a stretch; in fact, I recommend stretching. But use some reasoning behind your choices. (3) The affirmation must be stated in positive terms. For example, Muhammad Ali's trademark affirmation, "I am the greatest," has a much better ring to it than if he had said, "I am not a lousy boxer."

Research conducted by C. Jerry Downing, professor and chairperson of the Department of Counseling and Personnel Services at the University of Nevada, Reno, supports the validity of affirmations as transformational tools. His study indicates how positive affirmations can be used to build positive, self-fulfilling prophecies in children. While introducing the use of affirmations in eight schools, Downing found significant behavior change was often reported in a relatively short period of time when affirmations were specifically designed for the child and he or she was included in the actual writing process. In one example, a student who was having difficulty making friends worked with his counselor to write a series of six affirmations centering on how the student wanted to feel about himself. The student was asked to repeat each affirmation for approximately thirty seconds shortly after waking up in the morning and while showering in the evening. These were times he felt most relaxed and could count on privacy. Within weeks his relationships with other children were noticeably improved.

My client, Shauna, who had the conversation with money in the last chapter, had accumulated $40,000 worth of debt. She knew she had a problem. It was a constant weight on her mind, even though half of it was credit-card bills that she had consolidated into a home equity loan. For years she regularly wailed, "I'm $40,000 in debt! I've got $40,000 in debt, and I can't get rid of it!" As a result, she was stuck in the mind-set that her debt could never be decreased; she couldn't give herself a deadline and a plan to pay it off because she resented it so much.

One day I made a suggestion to Shauna: "Let's stop obsessing about the debt. We're clear on how much it is and what needs to be done. Instead, let's literally thank God for the opportunity to earn a substantial income and the ability to make payments every month. Bless each check as you write it out and bless each creditor's notice instead of cursing it!" Shauna immediately perked up, acknowledging that she'd been seeing this as a glass half empty, not half full. "After all, these creditors have trusted me and had confidence that I would repay," she said. "And I can live up to that!"

Shauna found power in her new "attitude of gratitude." She looked for reasons to be grateful even when she felt the burden of the debt she still carried and began using the affirmation *I am open to receiving the multitude of gifts and blessings that the Universe has for me.* She started out with the statement on index cards in her purse, on the bathroom mirror, and then put it on her screensaver. As she went about her workday, her computer constantly reminded her of the new behavior she wanted to embrace. Within a twelve-month period, she reduced her debt to $28,000 and was ecstatic about her progress.

Adopting a positive attitude and learning to view life's challenges as blessings is an important part of the financial healing process. But before we can work on changing our approach, we need to know exactly where we stand and what external factors—be they family, friends, the media, or the strangers we interact with on a daily basis—shape our spending habits and the way we relate to money. Determining your starting point will later help you gauge your ongoing financial progress and attitude adjustments. So be honest with yourself. Accept that you can't change what's happened in the past, but know that by looking at these deeply rooted patterns you can move beyond them into the future.

Exercise One: Recognize Your Emotions

Think about the times when you spend impulsively. What's usually going on in your life? Are you angry with your mate? Frustrated at work? Feeling sad, lonely, or inadequate? Take some time to complete the following sentences. Try to write at least one sheet of paper or one journal page for each statement. Write whatever comes to your mind and don't edit. See what is revealed to you in the process. If you get stuck, start the next sentence with "I feel" and continue to probe your thoughts and feelings about the statement.

I'm more likely to spend impulsively when _____.

Whenever I spend impulsively, I'm typically feeling _____.

The consequences of my impulse spending are usually_____.

Instead of spending impulsively I can choose to _____.

Exercise Two: Reflections of a Lifetime

What's your story? Think back over your adult life. How would you categorize the major periods of your life to date? In your journal or on a blank sheet of paper, take a few minutes to describe your financial life using three words or key phrases. For me, the terms *breakdown, breakout,* and *breakthrough* worked best. Just for fun, you might even try to summarize your life using song, television-program, or film titles. For example:

1. Shop Around [Smokey Robinson and the Miracles]. You indulged all your wants and needs.

2. Bills, Bills, Bills [Destiny's Child]. The results from your indulgence.

3. The Tracks of My Tears [Smokey Robinson and the Miracles]. The aftermath of emotions.

Exercise Three: Creating Inspirational Anchors

Internalizing positive affirmations is a big step toward taking action to break the tradition of money dysfunction passed on from generation to generation and getting your money straight. Don't hinder yourself or your children with money burdens any longer—declare that financial dysfunction stops with you! From here on in, use affirmations to anchor yourself to the new reality and belief system you want to create for your life.

First, identify five of your old beliefs that should be changed. For example: *I'll never get my bills paid off.* Next, determine the desired result—you want to be debt free. Now create a positive sentence, in the first person, present tense, that includes the desired result as if it has already been achieved. For example: *I radiate joy and share it with others as I live an abundant lifestyle free of debt.* Be sure to include powerful, inspirational words like *enthusiastic, magnificent, prosperous, dazzling, spectacular, marvelous, glorious, opulent, exciting, fantastic, splendid,* and *awesome.* These words help add energy to your affirmations. Read and contemplate each one for a minute in the morning and in the evening to start out. Do it aloud if possible. Use as much feeling as you can muster, and don't worry if it feels uncomfortable at first. That means only that you've touched upon an area that needs work.

After a while, increase the time for the ritual to five minutes and then to fifteen minutes. Know that repetition is a powerful way to reprogram your subconscious mind to accept these ideas as reality. Then be open and ready to experience a wonderful shift in your attitude and behavior.

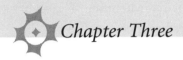 *Chapter Three*

Money in the Family

Although Suzanne* loved high fashion, she seldom shopped for new clothes. Instead, she stylishly coordinated the existing pieces in her wardrobe to maintain a fresh look. As a thirty-nine-year-old Internet consultant with no children, she appeared successful and professional as she drove around town in her used Acura. No one would have guessed that she had earned just $30,000 the previous year and was also $30,000 in debt.

The closer Suzanne got to her birthday and the "Big 4-0," the more she felt her life spinning out of control. Outwardly she appeared confident and presented a flawless image of perfect hair, nails, makeup,

---

* Suzanne isn't any one real person, but rather a composite of several of my clients.

and clothing. But inwardly she fought numerous demons, and the pain from the secrets she carried was often overwhelming. The reality was that she was heavily in debt and her credit report was full of delinquencies, charge-offs, and repossessions. She had lived for six years in a dysfunctional marriage and had just come to terms with having survived incest as a child. After years of faking it, she finally said, "My life has got to change before I turn forty. I have to stop the fantasy of how my world could be and look at how it really is."

When she took a hard look at her life, Suzanne realized that all these secrets—particularly the ones about her family and her childhood—were an enormous source of emotional distress that was affecting the way she managed her money. She began the monumental task of turning her life around by starting an intensive therapy program to help her deal with the psychological and emotional issues involved with leaving her marriage, confronting her childhood abuser, and informing her family of the childhood trauma. She then sought my help for financial counseling and, using my holistic approach, determined how to become financially self-sufficient while supporting and working through her emotional needs. Over a four-year period, Suzanne was able to give her life a full-scale makeover. After working through her family and money issues, she paid off her debts and created an annual income of $95,000 plus $20,000 in savings.

Bestselling author Iyanla Vanzant once poignantly described on *The Oprah Winfrey Show* how damaging it can be when we're "loyal to our family pattern," not realizing that "it's the family tree that has the noose around our neck." Most of us aren't even conscious of how influenced we are by our families. I frequently ask seminar participants, "How many of you had parents teach you about money—to make a budget, balance a checkbook, and so on?" Usually one percent or less of the group will raise their hands. Technically, they are correct. Most parents didn't sit us down at the kitchen table and directly teach us about finances. But our ideas about money don't come from nowhere. In reality, our families indirectly taught us a lot—from their attitudes regarding money and their financial practices. Bad money habits are passed on in families just like body types or the shape of one's eyes. In most cases, we either emulate their beliefs as we grow older or rebel and go 180 degrees in the opposite direction. Suzanne was no exception.

Suzanne's financial recovery was successful because she diligently followed the 7 Prescriptions I suggest in this book. But first she had to dig down to the core of her beliefs and understand how the messages she'd received as a child dictated the way she used money and created debt. To do that she traced her family's spending patterns back through history, using a genogram. A genogram is a diagram that records all the people in your family whose attitudes may have influenced your beliefs about money. It outlines all the players and helps you structurally document the emotions, behaviors, and lessons learned. Looking back at the different family dynamics can be hard, but it is all part of the healing process. At the end of this chapter—after I show you what Suzanne's family tree looks like—you'll create your own genogram to see if you've been acting out financially destructive scripts that were inherited from past generations.

Suzanne's Family Tree

Once Suzanne completed her family tree, I asked her to think about the psychological characteristics of each member of her family. I emphasized the importance of acknowledging everything she could remember even if it didn't seem to be relevant to finances. As she began her story, it seemed as though Suzanne had had a charmed childhood. She and her three siblings grew up in a predominantly white, middle-class neighborhood on Long Island. There were piano and tennis lessons and ballet recitals during her formative years, with plans for finishing school and a formal "coming-out" at a debutante ball in the future. For several years, her father had been a successful automobile salesman and was providing a pathway that relatively few others in our culture could afford toward black high society. "Mom and I would have tea and crumpets each afternoon at four o'clock when I arrived home after school," Suzanne said. "It was a very special time for us."

Suzanne's mother was very fashionable. She owned the best in clothes, jewelry, furs, and antiques and shopped at expensive department stores like Saks Fifth Avenue. She encouraged her children to strive for luxury homes, cars, and clothes, exciting travel, great food, and fine wine. Nothing was too good for her family because maintaining middle-class status was imperative. "My mother imagined herself to be the *black* Donna Reed," Suzanne said, tossing her head back with laughter as she thought about her mom on a typical day. "She tried to be the perfect wife, mother, and consummate homemaker in her crisply starched shirtwaist cotton dress with petticoat and three-inch high-heeled pumps to match." At the same time, this visually impressive and confident woman struggled with a great internal dichotomy—she had a feast-or-famine mentality and was fearful she could lose her security at any time. This was somewhat understandable, since she had never fully recovered from her father's death at an early age and the subsequent financial hardships imposed on her family. Because of this insecurity, Suzanne's mother was prone to keeping lots of cash in the house and would admit only to herself that she couldn't manage a checking account. Often she would say to Suzanne, "Don't ever let on that you're insecure about managing money."

Suzanne's father was financially a happy-go-lucky kind of guy because he came from money. Blessed with an upper-middle-class upbringing, he was indulged as a child and was used to having things given to him—from cashmere sweaters to his first car at age sixteen. His extravagant lifestyle grew as he became professionally successful as an adult and he, like Suzanne's mother, maintained an appreciation for the finer things in life. *Always strive to be a financial success* was a mantra that he followed. But Suzanne's dad didn't handle personal responsibility very well and eventually abused money and didn't pay his bills promptly. His actions dictated, "Buy what you want, when you want it, and pay the bills when it's convenient."

Suzanne's grandparents on both sides were hardworking people with whom she shared a warm and loving relationship. They had a strong work ethic and believed discipline and determination paid off whether as an employee or an entrepreneur. Her maternal grandfather was a carpenter by profession and died when Suzanne's mother was twelve. He left a small life insurance policy that provided for her maternal grandmother, who was a teacher. Suzanne and her grandmother had a close relationship until the time of her death when Suzanne was eighteeen. Her paternal grandparents were intelligent and savvy businesspeople. They owned land, income property, and grocery stores in the South. Over the years, they worked hard, became very prosperous, and tried to satisfy all the desires of their children and grandchildren.

During her childhood, Suzanne's family entertained frequently, and her mom enjoyed having cocktail parties and barbecues for friends and neighbors. Old family photographs captured her dad as the life of the party and found Mom chatting with guests, sociably poised with a martini glass in hand. What the photos didn't capture were the regular arguments and fights between her parents. On one occasion, her mother pulled a knife and threatened to kill her father when he came home drunk and became physically abusive. This led Suzanne to expect that chaos could break out on any given day. In this unstable home environment, she was always waiting for the other shoe to drop, and knew that there was financial insecurity with money because of the drinking and frivolous spending.

Over the years, alcohol consumption increased with her father and inevitably his business began to suffer. "It became increasingly more difficult for Dad to support our lavish lifestyle, which was already beyond his means," Suzanne said. Then she continued with sadness in her voice: "My parents' relationship continued to deteriorate, especially when Dad started leaving home for two and three days at a time." Before Suzanne turned eleven, her parents divorced and each remarried soon thereafter. Her stepmother was financially well-to-do and kept some of her finances separate from her new husband's. She was very generous with her family yet continued to tolerate Suzanne's father's frivolous spending. Her new stepfather was an attorney who also lived beyond his means, and a few years into the marriage an unexpected layoff created financial difficulty that eventually led him to file for bankruptcy. Suzanne's mother was devastated at the thought of this embarrassment and took every possible measure to ensure her family maintained the secret while they slowly reestablished themselves.

At the same time, Suzanne maintained a secret of her own. For a number of years she had been sexually abused by a male relative. As a child, in her attempts to please everyone, Suzanne endured several years of sexual abuse and incrementally more years of emotional damage and shame.

Together Suzanne and I assembled the pieces of the puzzle into a picture that reflected the reality of her life. Along with keeping up the appearance of wealth and social status, secrecy had been a major theme in her family. Suzanne had to keep the secret that they weren't good money managers; that they weren't as financially secure as they made themselves out to be; and that one of her relatives had spent years abusing her. Because of this, Suzanne had grown used to covering things up that made her feel scared or ashamed, so it wasn't surprising that her debt had gotten so out of control and she kept it hidden.

Ironically Suzanne had been encouraged by her biological parents to be independent and financially secure. But through their actions, the real message seemed to be "Find someone with financial means who can take care of you." As a result, Suzanne was very conflicted. She recognized her need to be financially secure, but total independence was scary and frightening, and at heart she believed that "financial independence means I'll be alone and lonely." So although she developed a successful Internet consulting practice, Suzanne focused on finding a suitable husband rather than on pushing her business to its fullest potential. She married a successful dentist and her upscale lifestyle of fabulous homes and luxury cars continued. Her wedding was a major event of the season, with eight bridesmaids and a sit-down dinner for two hundred guests.

After a three-week honeymoon in Africa, the newlyweds returned to the States expecting a lifetime of abundance. But within three years, her husband's business fell apart and Suzanne was left with $30,000 worth of debt to deal with on her own. She was angry with him for the business failure and angry with herself for not being able to save him. Eventually their relationship grew hostile. After being forced out of her home by the threat of foreclosure and having her car repossessed, Suzanne again felt like the other shoe had dropped and she was left feeling insecure and unsafe once more.

Only after confronting her sexual abuser and informing her family of what had transpired in her childhood did Suzanne begin to release the shame-filled burden that contributed to her low self-worth. The revelation freed her of self-hatred and she started believing she could have a prosperous life without chaos. Suzanne realized her internal self-esteem was more important than external images, and she adjusted her lifestyle to meet her income. By systematically using the principles outlined in this book, she followed a program of debt reduction and planned spending. Most important, she was able to eliminate the damaging financial habits inherited from her family and internalize new, healthy messages that rebuilt her self worth and net worth.

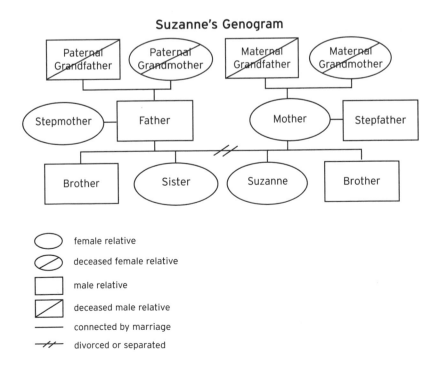

Suzanne's Genogram

◯	female relative
⬭ (crossed)	deceased female relative
▭	male relative
▱ (crossed)	deceased male relative
——	connected by marriage
‑//‑	divorced or separated

Below are the significant memories Suzanne gleaned from her history as she reflected on the financial and emotional characteristics of her family members:

Suzanne's Family
Mother
- Maintaining middle-class status was imperative
- Owned the best in clothes, jewelry, furs, and antiques
- Enjoyed cocktail parties and socializing
- Insecure regarding money; couldn't manage checking account
- Kept lots of cash in the house
- Feast-or-famine mentality

Father
- Upper-middle-class childhood
- Was indulged as a child
- Had an extravagant lifestyle as an adult
- Abused money and didn't pay bills
- A drinker

Stepfather
- Made good money but lived beyond means
- Unexpected layoff created financial difficulty; eventually filed bankruptcy

Stepmother
- Financially well-to-do
- Generous and enabling

Maternal Grandfather
- A carpenter by profession
- Died when Suzanne's mother was twelve
- Left a small insurance policy

Maternal Grandmother
- A teacher by profession
- Died when Suzanne was eighteen
- Had a warm, loving relationship with Suzanne

Paternal Grandfather
- An intelligent and shrewd businessman
- Owned land and income property

Paternal Grandmother
- Helped her husband with business
- Indulged her children and grandchildren

Based on these characteristics, below are the internalized messages and beliefs that Suzanne absorbed from prior generations of her family:

From Mother
- Status, money, and security are most important.
- Strive for luxury homes, cars, clothes, travel, great food, and fine wine.
- Don't let on that you're insecure managing money.
- Security can be taken away at any time.

From Father
- Appreciate the finer things in life.
- Always strive to be a financial success.
- Buy what you want, when you want it, and pay the bills when it's convenient.

From Maternal and Paternal Grandparents
- Work hard and provide the best for your family.
- Discipline and determination pay off whether you're an employee or an entrepreneur.

From Stepfather
- Planning is important, but it's still possible to live beyond your means.
- You can reestablish yourself after financial devastation.

From Stepmother
- Keep some credit cards in your own name.
- Be generous with friends and family.

Common Family Messages That Cause Problems

The genograms of other clients have revealed a host of equally problematic beliefs that are passed down from one generation to the next. Check off how many of those mentioned in the next section your mother or other female relatives taught you—either by word or deed, which, as we know, are not always the same thing.

Keep a Lil' Cash on the Side That He Doesn't Know About

Mama's well-meaning message is meant as a protective mechanism to help her daughters take care of themselves and not be totally dependent on a man. "Always have mad money," Suzanne's mother would exhort, "because a man will act a fool over money." As we've already seen, there were lots of issues between her parents and lots of discord in their household, so the saying "God bless the child who has [her] own" had a particularly special meaning to Suzanne's mom, and it's not surprising she'd encourage her daughter to have a slush fund.

For generations, black women have been very creative in establishing their little stash of cash. We have been known for "squeezing the blood out of a turnip" and "making a way when there was no way." Some have rolled up cash and put it in a special pair of socks in the sock drawer. Some have stuffed cash and a credit card in the little black purse in the back of the closet, just in case they need to unexpectedly stay overnight in a hotel. One thirty-year-old sister in my focus group recalled how her grandmother told her, "Keep some cash in a Kotex box. He'll never look for it in there!"

The power in Mama and Grandma's message has led many a black woman to become financially independent, which is good. But carrying secrets and having a lack of trust can cripple the relationship of an African American couple, setting a tone for dishonesty, and that tone can permeate into other areas of the marriage. Sometimes sisters believe "my money is my money, but his money is our money." Or couples have no idea how much money their spouses make, so the separation of finances and the inability to communicate effectively about money keeps it a taboo subject of discussion and makes it difficult if not impossible to work toward common goals. The 4 C's of Couples and Money presented later in this book provide guidelines for enhancing communication skills about finances.

Be the Responsible One

The "responsibility" pressure starts early in most black women's lives. Female children are conditioned to be "good girls" and to take responsibility for everything. In the black family, if you get in trouble (pregnant), you might be told, "That's your problem!" or "You made your bed, now lie in it!" We're pressed to get a good education, a good job, and make money, but the pressure can be a lot for even the strongest, most resourceful sister to handle.

In many cases, we're the first generation of college graduates and sometimes make more money than both parents combined. This can be tough if other family members become resentful or start turning to us as the family bank, an endless source of monetary handouts and help. We feel guilty for being in a better position than our family members and may ultimately end up shouldering their financial responsibilities for them. But by bailing them out of each emergency, and trying to be the responsible provider, we sometimes jeopardize our own financial stability.

It's a very easy situation to get drawn into. In the years before my own financial collapse, I would periodically receive a telephone call from a relative in desperate need of $200 or $300 because he was short on the rent payment. I'd immediately know that I didn't have the cash and could have turned him down for that reason. But I also knew I had something he didn't have—available credit—and I could simply take a cash advance on my credit card to fix the situation. Looking back now, it never occurred to me to make it a *loan* and have him pay the money back to my account. I focused only on how I was a bank manager, supposedly doing well, living in California, and should be in a position to help those in my family who needed it.

There are many variations on how black women feel responsible for others and weaken our finances in the process. After years of giving money to needy relatives, my client Shauna found a different but equally destructive way to handle the problem. She simply got rid of her money before they asked! Shauna was considered a successful woman by all her relatives. She was single, had a great job, and owned her own home. But she always felt she was just getting by even though she consistently earned a good income. "Eventually I rationalized, if I spent the money on myself before they asked, I could legitimately say, 'Sorry, I don't have any money' to anyone who even hinted they were in need." By indulging herself with clothes and vacations, Shauna spent all her money—and then some—before hitting rock bottom by accumulating $40,000 worth of debt. At that point, the relatives were the least of her economic worries.

"There's nothing harder for a black woman than to reach out and get support," says Dr. Brenda Wade. "She has to accept that she needs it, that she deserves it, and then she must take action to get it." As we work on getting our money straight, it's important to realize that being responsible means being responsible for *you*—not for everybody else.

You're Not Good Enough

Sometimes it's the unspoken family messages that can do the most damage. For my client Lee, compulsive spending through mail-order catalogues was a remedy for hurt feelings that escalated over time into a full-blown addiction. By ordering hundreds of items such as fancy dishes, kitchen appliances, clothes, and shoes, Lee found a way to numb emotional pain. Her purchases were so numerous and frequent that she'd lose track of what she ordered. When the items arrived in the mail, they were like unexpected gifts. Hurtful feelings and emotional pain were so prevalent in Lee's life that one year, when her husband was out of town on their wedding anniversary, Lee purchased a fur coat that she could ill afford because she felt neglected and abandoned. But this behavior was minimal compared to the secret Lee carried from day to day: Over a two-and-a-half-year period, Lee had systematically spent her family's $25,000 savings and created an additional $12,000 in debt while trying to nurture her emotional voids and handle her family's basic expenses.

When Lee began reflecting on her history, it was easy to locate the root of the problem. She was just eight months old when her father left his family. Lee's father, however, had developed a close relationship with her older sister before he left, and each subsequent year lavished her with gifts while ignoring Lee. This emotional deprivation made Lee feel that she wasn't good enough to merit her father's attention. His lack of acknowledgment and unavailability made her feel unworthy and undeserving. As a child, she was never able to express her feelings about this neglect and never able to confront her father. Lee grew into adulthood avoiding conflict and confrontation, not just with her father but with everyone. She was never able to articulate her anger and dismay when people around her did hurtful things. Whenever she became angry or depressed, she would deal with her feelings by spending money, giving herself the material possessions she had longed for as a child.

Not having the emotional support she desperately needed helped to feed Lee's sense of deprivation. Fortunately, with my encouragement, Lee finally admitted to her husband the information she'd withheld over a thirty-month period and revealed the resulting state of their finances. "Coming clean" helped Lee avoid a near nervous breakdown. Upon learning what his wife had done, Lee's husband was furious and for a while their marriage hovered on the brink of divorce. But over time they were able to work things out by identifying the deep-seated emotional pain that they both had carried from their childhoods and by learning how to develop a balanced spending plan that accounted for both needs *and* wants.

Because some messages are nonverbal, they aren't as obvious to detect. The emotional void created by her father's lack of attention developed into emotional deprivation that Lee tried to fill with "stuff." Over time, Lee learned to resist the "you're not good enough" messages she had received and choose other paths to emotional fulfillment. In learning how to love herself, she was able to modify her spending and improve her family's finances.

Do More for Your Children Than I Was Able to Do for You

When I have the opportunity to spend time with my three young nephews, ages four, five, and six, I usually end up worn out and exhausted from playing tag, giving "horsey" rides, playing twenty questions, and responding to forty-five minutes or so of continuous knock-knock jokes. It's then that I'm reminded that parenting is one of the most challenging and rewarding experiences a person can have, twenty-four hours a day, seven days a week, for life!

The closest I've come to the parental experience was with my dog, Blood, who thought he was my child. He had his own room, always got new chew toys and doggie treats when I went to the store, ate the best foods, and had the best veterinarians and dog trainers. After my divorce, I came close to making a decision of choosing a house that met his needs and not mine. Talk about codependent! If I could go to this extreme over a dog, I can well imagine the degree to which parents will go to have the best for their kids.

Some African American parents were indulged and spoiled as children. But providing the same type of lifestyle for their offspring may not necessarily create a normal, healthy environment for their kids' growth. Often money is squandered on things that have limited use or appeal to children. For instance, how essential is it to buy Air Jordans for a two-year-old child or to have a garage so full of toys, you're forced to park your car on the driveway?

Those of us who weren't spoiled as children try to make a special effort to make sure our kids have all the advantages we may have missed out on when we were young. We'd like to provide our children with an abundant lifestyle, but instead many hardworking parents struggle on a daily basis to just make ends meet. Trying to save money with school-age kids in the household often seems impossible. Among the financial challenges parents face are dealing with enormous monthly food expenses, kids quickly growing out of everything, and peer pressure for the latest designer fashions and popular toys.

Young people today are as consumed with instant gratification and material things as are adults. Black kids are especially at risk because of the "fast money" opportunities they see in their neighborhoods, like selling drugs and gambling as a way to obtain material status symbols. All the more reason why the role of the black parent is critical in instilling steadfast values, appropriate respect, and responsible money management habits in their children.

In wanting a better life for their families, some parents are in a position to enroll their children in private schools, while others move to "better" communities (usually white), where the public school system is far superior to the urban classroom and neighborhoods are safer. Kids in these communities are often enrolled in a variety of after-school classes, including music, tennis, soccer, golf, swimming, gymnastics, computers, and special tutoring programs, to name a few. While they will certainly enhance your child's education, these courses can be costly when added to normal expenditures like food, shelter, clothing, child care, and braces—let alone pleas for Star Wars and Pokémon characters. Believe it or not, excessive spending on children—while it may make you and them happy—may not be the best thing for them, especially if you can't really afford it in the long run.

As a parent, you need to explore the values and motivations behind this kind of spending. Are you doing it for the child's benefit or to compensate for your own childhood deprivations? Many of today's black parents grew up not necessarily impoverished but far from comfortable. Their parents provided the basic necessities and some extras, like toys and clothes for birthdays and Christmas. But often, as children, they still desired more and better-quality things. Sometimes kids were forced to get part-time jobs starting at age twelve or thirteen to earn money for clothes and day-to-day spending. Having worked continuously since that time, many adults are resentful and don't want their kids to have the same experience. It's very natural and noble to want to give our youngsters the best of everything—but it's not always right.

The challenge for today's parents is to keep things in perspective and know when excessive spending is rooted in our old emotional needs rather than in the needs of our children. We must learn to say no to ourselves as well as to our offspring, regardless of how painful it may feel. If parents give too much and make things too easy, not only can it strain the family finances, it can hamper the child's ability to function in the real world. Overindulgence and constant rescuing creates a crutch that prohibits the child's development of independent life skills. It may also create a false sense of reality of what is necessary to lead a happy and healthy life.

Adult children who can't seem to make it on their own is one problem many mothers face. Kids who are always asking for loans and bailouts didn't learn the lessons of financial responsibility early on. If your pattern is to provide for them each time they are in need, you are establishing a counterproductive blueprint for your children, grandchildren, and great-grandchildren to follow. Once I saw an interview with actress Halle Berry, who described a traumatic experience early on in her acting career. Halle was broke and needed money for food and rent, so she called home. Her mom, who was having some financial difficulty at the time, could have scraped together some money to help her daughter, but instead she said no. Distraught and dismayed, Halle didn't speak to her mother for a year and a half. Today, however, she admits saying no was the best thing her mother could have done because it helped her become independent and take responsibility for her financial survival. Now a huge success and one of the most sought-after actresses in Hollywood, Halle doesn't need financial support from Mom and has even bought her mother a fabulous lakefront home in the Midwest.

The single black female parent has added pressures in that she often feels alone, lost, and overwhelmed. Many are everyday working moms with inconsistent or nonexistent child support. These sisters are forced to try to compensate emotionally and financially for the lack of a father in their child's life. African American mothers with male children have special concerns, since boys are more at risk of dropping out of school and getting involved in drugs and gangs. One client, Celeste, worked hard and spent considerable money buying her son things. His room was well put together with everything he needed and most of what he wanted. It was practical and functional for a nine-year-old. Celeste also involved her son in numerous extracurricular activities and classes. These efforts to keep him occupied and out of trouble cost her $400 per month just for transportation!

Since Celeste didn't have a husband or partner to share the responsibility with, she was forced to hire someone to transport the boy to and from school, basketball practice, tutoring sessions, and all other weekday activities. Celeste felt she didn't have a choice and that it was necessary to absorb this additional expense because her average workday, including commute time, was seven A.M. to seven P.M. Aside from the fact that these expenses put her in a financial bind, Celeste had scheduled so many activities that one weekend her son finally said, "Mom, can we just stay home?" In her efforts to fill his life, Celeste not only stretched herself thin financially but sacrificed priceless mother-child quality time.

Another single parent I know, Imani, developed a wonderfully creative way to teach her five-year-old daughter about money and keep herself financially on track. They play the money game. After cashing her paycheck each week, Imani and her daughter go home, spread a blanket on the floor, and then proceed to sort the money out in piles: a separate pile for rent, food, gasoline, telephone, utilities, child care, savings, and so on. Imani then gently explains to her daughter: "Now, see, honey, sometimes when you ask Mommy for things and I say no, it's not because I'm being mean or that I don't love you. It's because there just isn't always money left over." This simple exercise also served to remind Imani of their strict budget, and how careful she needed to be with their spare change.

Imani later told me of an incident that verified how even a five-year-old can grasp the concept of money management. Her daughter, while riding in the car with her auntie, overheard the aunt say how she planned to borrow some money from Imani for gasoline. Imani's daughter chimed in from the backseat, "Oh, no, don't ask my mommy for money because we're saving for a house! If you need money for gas, I'll loan you some from my piggy bank!"

As always, profound statements come from the mouths of babes! It just goes to show that we sometimes underestimate the intelligence and supportiveness of our children when we fail to discuss money with them openly. We also deny them critical values and financial education. By the way, Imani and her daughter did later purchase a beautiful home and are doing quite well financially.

Couples and Money

Many black women today have not waited for a husband to provide for their financial security. We have achieved the American dream of owning our homes along with the other trappings of success based on the message of independence that we heard—be strong, be independent, and take care of yourself. And that's a good thing. But be aware that brothers are also heard frequently to say, "Well, if you have all that, what do you need me for?" If you are currently in a relationship, developing an open, productive dialogue with your partner about money is one of the major steps to getting your finances straight.

If money is a major issue or bone of contention between a couple, chances are that money is not the real problem in the relationship. Ongoing arguments and fights about money are just the symptom or the excuse for the discord. In most cases, issues of power and control are at the root of money conflicts. If a woman feels that her partner is trying to exert excessive control over her life, she may rebel by spending excessively. "I work hard and I'll buy what I want" is a familiar claim from black women. "Nobody's going to tell me what to do or how to spend my money." Even if she has to do it secretively by hiding new purchases in the trunk of her car, a woman will use her "buying power" to exert a sense of power that she may not feel in other areas of her relationship. The more she may feel controlled by her partner, the more she may spend to excess. This in turn causes the partner to become more controlling, which leads to more rebellion, and the dance continues with all parties ultimately being unsatisfied, unhappy, and potentially financially wrecked.

As we saw in Chapter Two, some women are caught up in the same dysfunction that I was with Jeffrey—unconsciously trying to buy love and affection from a partner or spouse. Or some women, in an effort to be supportive, end up "supporting" their partners. They take on too much responsibility and end up paying for too much. Other women believe in very traditional roles where the man is the breadwinner and thus the wife shouldn't have to pay for entertainment expenses or household expenditures once married. If they happen to work, such women feel their money is their own. It's important to recognize the individual dynamics that are at work within your particular relationship.

In my ten years of experience as a financial recovery specialist, I've found that men are less likely than women to acknowledge shortcomings in their financial management. Black men are no exception. But in an effort to help sisters everywhere know where their men are coming from, I did an informal, unscientific survey to gain insight into men's attitudes about women and money.

Suffice it to say there are all kinds of people out there whom you can date and eventually marry. In general, opposites attract—that is, savers are more likely to hook up with spenders. I talked to brothers ranging from easygoing and generous with their money to those who are angry and resentful because they feel they've been taken advantage of. I have heard lots of horror stories on both sides of the equation. The truth is: Not all men are gigolos and not all women are gold diggers. Nor are all women spendthrifts, or all men good money managers.

Here are some of the common insights from the men:

- When couples are young and neither the men nor the women have much money, it's usually not too difficult to talk about finances. As we become older, we become more uncomfortable and embarrassed when we compare where we are with where we think we should be. We don't want the other person to know that we haven't done better with our money.

- Because of generally accepted social mores, if a woman says, "I'd like to see you tonight," and suggests getting together to do something, brothers believe they will be expected to pay for the date. They tend to expect that the woman will pay for the date only if she says something up front like "I want to take you out" or "I have tickets for the D'Angelo concert and I would like to invite you."

- If a brother invites a sister out on a date, he doesn't expect that she will pay for any part of it, but it would be nice on occasion, say, after the third or fourth date, if she at least offered to leave a tip.

Clarity and communication are the key elements to couples maintaining financial harmony. Having an up-front dialogue can eliminate many potential money problems. For instance, when planning a trip together or a getaway, if he's not intending to foot the total bill, a brother prefers to decide in advance who will pay for what. Especially when it comes to the big-ticket items. He might say, "Don't worry about the airfare. I'll take care of it. You can pay for the hotel and we'll split the meals" or "We'll each contribute $200 to the pot and that will pay for our meals." On occasions when these things are not cleared in advance, it makes for a very uncomfortable and ugly trip.

Couples should get over the idea that "if we need to talk about money, you don't trust me or you don't really love me." As you move forward with this book's program, talking about money with your partner will be essential. Be prepared to compromise and don't think that love will take care of everything, because it won't.

Exercise One: Get Yourself Centered

Like Suzanne, you can understand and make the connection between conscious and unconscious internalized messages that govern your current money-management behaviors. As you prepare to complete the upcoming exercises, you should consider the financial and emotional status of your parents and grandparents when they were between ages thirty and fifty. This is the age range when most responsible adults become serious about life and their accomplishments to date. They've moved beyond the first job, car, and apartment and have hopefully established themselves. Before we get started, take a moment, close your eyes, and breathe in deeply several times. Allow yourself to get grounded and centered. Ask God or whatever source you use for spiritual guidance to open your heart and your head to recall the imperative messages without prescreening.

Exercise Two: Diagram Your Family Tree

Now you're ready to diagram a few generations of your family tree. Feel free to expand beyond the basic relatives, especially if there were aunts, uncles, and cousins who were influential in your childhood. Let's start with your generation. You will need a large piece of paper. Once you have it, start by plotting yourself and each of your siblings:

> You
> Your siblings
> Your mother
> Your father
> Your maternal grandparents
> Your paternal grandparents

If you like, add your great-grandparents. You may not have known them, but think about what you've heard from your parents and grandparents about the way they handled their finances.

Now that we have all the characters in place, let's look for spoken and unspoken messages. For example, a common saying like "Money is the root of all evil" can become an internalized belief that "money is bad." (By the way, the actual quote is "the *love* of money is the root of all evil.") Either way, such messages may make you think such thoughts as "If I make too much money, I'll be bad" or "Being poor is more virtuous." Thinking like that can block you from pursuing your full financial potential and make you feel undeserving of a good salary.

Now take a separate sheet of paper and fold it in half vertically. List each relative's name in the left-hand column, leaving five or six lines between each, to record words and phrases that describe their attitudes, beliefs, feelings, and behaviors related to money. Use additional sheets of paper if necessary. List everyone on your genogram, except yourself. We'll get back to you later.

Next, consider the following questions as you list below each name the significant facts for that person or family group. Don't panic—you don't have to answer every question for each individual. Simply use these questions to get to the essence of their behavioral patterns.

Sample Questions

- What was the overall financial status of each family?
- Were they in poverty? Struggling day to day? In survival mode? Heavily indebted?
- Did they live comfortably? Or even large?
- Did they have enough food to eat?
- Were bills paid on time?

- Did they have money in the bank?
- Were retirement plans secure?
- Did they rent or own their home? Was it in a safe and secure neighborhood?
- Did they own any income property or have other investments?
- Were they able to leave money or property to their children?
- Were they able to travel?
- Were they wage earners or entrepreneurs?
- What type of work did they do? Professional, labor, or service-oriented?
- Were they steadily employed?
- What was the level of education?
- Who controlled the money in the household? What was their attitude?
- Could they financially help other family members when in need?
- Did they have insurance or have to scrape together money for burial expenses if someone died?
- Is there any history of eviction, bankruptcy, repossession, foreclosure, or financial ruin? Was it business or personal?
- Were they ever on welfare or public assistance? If so, why and for how long?
- Were they married, single, or in relationships? How did they feel about that status?
- Who experienced divorce and what was the major problem in the marriage?
- Were relationships nurturing, supportive, indifferent, or abusive?
- How were relationships with other family members?
- Relationships with other people in general?
- Did anyone marry into money? Did anyone marry into poverty?
- Were there abuses, addictive behavior, or fanaticism?
- Was there excessive eating, drinking, gambling, drugs, sex, or religion?
- What was their general attitude about life? Optimistic or pessimistic?
- Did they feel oppressed and discriminated against?
- Did they have a positive attitude about money? A prosperity consciousness?
- Did they have a high or low level of self-esteem?
- What were their favorite sayings or messages?
- Was anyone a codependent, major caretaker, or enabler?
- Were they fearful or anxious?
- Did they believe "There's not enough" or "There's never enough"?
- Did they argue or fight about money? Were they secretive about money?

- Were they embarrassed, shameful, or guilt-ridden about finances?
- Did they shame or guilt-trip others? Did they have a "you-owe-me" type of attitude?
- Were there any other traumatic events affecting finances or self-worth?

Now let's use the right side of the page to respond to each characteristic you listed on the left side. Use Suzanne's genogram analysis as a guide. How do you relate to each point? How did you internalize your family's beliefs and attitudes? For example: Based on these attitudes, you now believe that blacks always get the short end of the stick or that we always have to struggle in life. How do your behaviors with money emulate or oppose theirs? Finally, look over your responses and write one paragraph summarizing what traits, patterns, and beliefs have passed down through the generations of your family—both positive and negative. Acknowledge yourself for being honest and forthright about your family and indicate what aspects or areas you'd like to change in yourself.

Exercise Three: Confronting the Past

Prepare to write two letters, one to your parents and one to society in general. Keep in mind, these letters are not going to be mailed. They are simply an opportunity for you to identify and vent any anger, resentment, sadness, or disappointment that may be blocking you from getting your money straight and becoming self-assured and self-confident with your finances. Writing letters is an amazingly helpful way to purge and eliminate feelings of insecurity and inadequacy.

These are not ordinary letters and will not be written in an ordinary way. So let's start by getting the proper stationery—a roll of toilet paper! That's right! Toilet paper. Not because it's practical for letter writing, but because it's very practical for our "release" process. After completing the letter, we're going to dispose of the limiting beliefs and disempowering experiences by flushing them away and out of your life. Start by personalizing your letter: Dear Mama or Dear Daddy. Use a ballpoint pen to ensure easy writing. Now read the following questions and ponder the thoughts and emotions they bring up. Take as much time as you need and write down all of your feelings and observations:

- How were your emotional needs unmet as you were growing up?
- What would you have liked your parents to say or do to nurture you better?
- In what ways were you shown conditional love as opposed to unconditional love?
- What incidents from family and society have made you feel less than adequate? For example:
    - A relative who constantly said your sister was "the pretty one" because she was light-skinned
    - A school counselor who said you should become a nurse because you weren't smart enough or could never become a doctor
    - An employer who promoted the blue-eyed, blond-haired, incompetent coworker
- How has the media perpetuated images to diminish your self-worth? For example:
    - The pervasive image on television that women of European descent are the standard of beauty for the world
    - Consistent use of the word "black" to describe negative events— for instance, the stock market crash as "Black Monday"

After completing the letters, reread them, and make sure you've tapped into all the emotions that had previously been minimized, avoided, saved up, or suppressed, and put them on paper. Once this is done, devise a ritual where you release the letters by flushing them down the toilet, tearing them up and putting them in the trash, or burning them in the fireplace. Say a prayer to let go of any feelings and attitudes that block you from knowing that you are worthy and deserving. Forgive and bless all those involved who made you feel less than adequate and forgive yourself for allowing the experiences to affect you. As you see the letters disappear, visualize all the negative energy related to these feelings going away as well. Feel any residual heaviness leave your body. Now take a deep breath, praise yourself, and let the new, lighter, uplifted you go forward with confidence as you continue to work on getting your money straight!

Exercise Four: Creating Common Ground

Make no mistake about it. Whether you are in a relationship or not, there are some important questions to ask yourself in order to get financial clarity and to set goals. Having this knowledge also helps you gauge your willingness to work with a partner on financial objectives. If you have a mate, each of you should respond to the questions in writing. Then schedule at least two hours when the two of you are relaxed and available to discuss your answers. The questions address the 4 C's of Couples and Money:

1. Clarity—Before commingling finances and addressing joint household needs, each individual must be very clear about where he or she stands financially on a personal level. What do you own? What do you owe? Is your checkbook balanced? What does your credit report look like? What are your saving habits? What are your spending habits? What are your attitudes and values about money? What are your financial goals?

2. Communication—In any successful relationship, communication is key. Are you willing to discuss openly and honestly the questions about finances indicated above without criticism, anger, or judgment? Are you willing to take the time and energy to plan, track, and analyze your family's finances?

3. Compromise—Once the necessary issues are brought to the table, each person needs to feel he or she contributed to the discussion and must buy into the decision. Are you willing to give a little and take a little in order to create a win/win financial situation?

4. Commitment—There must be a commitment from each party to make any financial plan work. Each person must be open and honest with respect to his or her concerns, fears, and feelings. Are you willing to commit to the relationship and commit to the process of joint management of finances?

Exercise Five: Teaching Financial Values

For generations money has been a taboo subject in most families, so many young people have no idea what it takes to provide themselves with the lifestyle to which they've become accustomed. In early adulthood, they face culture shock as the reality sets in as to how much money it takes to provide oneself with food, shelter, and clothing. This exercise is to begin family dialogue on money matters, goal setting, and the establishment of family objectives. Encourage input and support from all household members. Also, before starting, make sure you've completed the 4 C's of Couples and Money exercise to ensure that both you and your mate have common objectives.

1. Schedule a family financial meeting to discuss the current financial status and family goals.

2. Keep a relaxed atmosphere. Don't criticize or place blame on anyone for financial problems. No need to be too detailed. Kids don't need to be burdened with the total amount of outstanding family debt.

3. Talk about the type of lifestyle you want for your family. Ask the kids to describe what they'd like their life to look like. Establish a common goal to work toward—for example, something as large as a new house or as small as a new VCR.

4. Explain that, as a family, with proper planning, discipline, patience, and God's help you can achieve the goal.

5. Now look at the reality of the current financial situation. Detail your income versus expenses. Keep it light. Make a game of it. Start by asking, "How much money do you kids think we have to work with on a monthly basis?" After hearing several guesses, write the actual amount on a piece of paper. Then ask, "How much money do you think our house payment is?" Again, after hearing several guesses, write down the actual amount and subtract it from the net income figure. Continue down the list, subtracting your other monthly expenses.

6. Finally, assure your family, as Imani did in an earlier anecdote, that if you have to say no to some of their requests, it's not because you don't love them. Remind them that their basic needs will be met as well as some of their wants, but their assistance and support is needed to achieve the family goal that you've all agreed on.

 *Part Two*

Seven Prescriptions for Financial Health and Healing

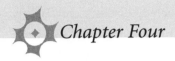img

Chapter Four

Prescription 1:
Set Goals That Speak
to Your Heart

Every January 1, my intentions were always good as I made my New Year's resolutions. I'd focus on the new and improved Glinda that I wanted to become and would create a list of the changes I wanted to make. I'm not alone. I'm sure many of you sisters join in the annual ritual of making verbal promises and proclamations to seek healthy relationships, cut back on eating sweets, achieve the perfect weight, and the ever-popular pay off bills. But when the January start date gets reset to February and then February to March, we become discouraged and end up saying "Just forget it." That's the closest some of us ever get to setting goals.

For the last decade or so, I've had a lot of explaining to do to friends in early January because I want to prepare them for the unusual behavior I'm likely to exhibit over the course of the month. During this period, I'm sure to be distracted, distant, and largely unavailable. (Thankfully, I now have the process whittled down from thirty days to two or three.) In actuality, what is taking place is the annual ritual of redesigning my life.

As I begin each year, I like to get quiet, go within, and reflect on what I want my life to look like for the next twelve months. I don't stop my financial counseling practice, but I take care of only the most pressing commitments. I inform friends that I am available only in case of emergency, and I avoid anything that might distract me from the mindfulness of my annual goal-setting process.

Getting quiet to think about what's fundamentally important to me is a key part of creatively "designing my life." I actually visualize a blank canvas and begin to mentally paint a picture of how I want the upcoming year to look. I paint a lifestyle that is fun, exciting, and meets every wish my heart desires. In my mind's eye, I assess where I'm currently at and then take it up a notch or two to the next level. For example, on the professional side, I might visualize myself with an upgraded working wardrobe. So I'll see myself facilitating a seminar in a beautiful St. John knit suit—moving about the room interacting with attendees, looking good, feeling confident, and having fun. Or I might visualize having a car service pick me up at the airport instead of taking a shuttle or taxi to the hotel when I travel for pleasure, not just for business trips. Once I have the vision clarified, I set my goals.

Believe it or not, this visualization process helped me learn to make my goals a reality. Setting appropriate goals and then staying on track until you achieve them takes patience and discipline. It's a skill that every sister has to learn if we're going to get our money straight. Maybe you're already used to setting goals and meeting them—if so, good for you. But if you have trouble accomplishing the things you want in life—financial or otherwise—perhaps you need to rethink your goal-setting process. That way you can make certain you aren't setting yourself up for failure before you actually get started. The following multiple-choice quiz will help you determine if your goal-setting procedures doom you to failure or destine you for success. Pick one response to complete each sentence:

1. It's important to have a reason why you want to accomplish a goal because:
   a. Your mother always said you'd better have a good excuse for what you do.
   b. A reason will help you stay disciplined and motivated to accomplish the goal.
   c. Your mentor suggested it.

2. You know you have chosen the right goal if:
   a. Your coworker tells you so.
   b. It's the "in" thing you read about in a magazine.
   c. It's a burning desire and it speaks to your heart.

3. Each goal you select should be:
   a. Clearly defined and measurable, with action steps and a target date.
   b. Something you have always wanted.
   c. Discussed at length with your sisterfriends.

4. To have balance in your overall life plan, you should:
   a. Delegate as much as possible.
   b. Create personal and professional goals.
   c. Make sure your family tells you what they need from you.

5. Establishing financial benchmarks for each decade helps you:
   a. Determine how badly to beat yourself up if you miss a goal.
   b. Aim higher than you ordinarily do.
   c. Plan your lifetime needs and determine how early you may want to retire.

6. Adding elements like prayer and meditation to your lifestyle can help you:
   a. Express gratitude for your blessings.
   b. Maintain perspective on the source of your good fortune.
   c. Alleviate paralyzing fear when financial challenges occur.
   d. All of the above.

Answers: b, c, a, b, c, d

How did you do? Hopefully, you answered all the questions correctly. Obviously, they weren't designed for you to need a Ph.D. to answer them. Instead, they were set up to be used as an outline for the components of Prescription 1, which will help you set goals that make your heart sing and get you started down the road to a peaceful relationship with your money.

Query 1: What's Your Burning Desire?

A critical part of a successful financial program is having a goal or objective that motivates and energizes you. It's not enough to just say "I want to be debt free" or "I want to save money." Having a compelling reason *why* you want to become debt free or a motivating goal for which you are saving money creates a burning desire that gives you the motivation to go forward when you get tired and frustrated or when you feel you're not progressing fast enough. And because you're a human being, you're destined to feel all of these things from time to time.

Some sisters put off dealing with finances until they're in a serious relationship and discussing marriage. With the engagement comes shame and guilt as they think, "Oh, God, now he'll find out I've got all these bills!" That's when they panic. My client, Florence, was admittedly an impulsive spender, but a new man in her life and a marriage proposal made her determined to wipe out her debt.

At age twenty-six, Florence had traveled more in five years than most people do in a lifetime. In the beginning she was nervous about setting out on some of her global adventures to places like Sierra Leone, Costa Rica, and Hong Kong. A black woman traveling alone is a rarity. But Florence quickly got over her fear. "I've practically been around the world," she said. "I've learned so much about different cultures, I'd say it was worth every penny." Unfortunately, those pennies totaled in the millions. This young single woman, who worked as a physical therapist earning $70,000 a year, had no savings and owed $31,000 on her car, $9,000 on her credit cards, $60,000 in student loans, and $7,000 in family loans.

Getting engaged prompted Florence to take a serious reality check. The early conversations about money with Russell, her fiancé, called her attention to the frivolous spending patterns she had developed. She also realized that Russell, a divorced man with two children, was a good money manager. He had clean credit, minimal debt, was buying a home, and was saving for his kids' education.

Reluctant to disclose the specifics of her situation, Florence acknowledged to her fiancé that she had more debt than she was comfortable with and was determined to get her financial act together. She told me: "Russell offered to help me with my finances, but I'm not ready for him to see them yet. Plus, I don't think it would be good for our relationship for him to be monitoring my spending. I want him to be proud of me, so I have to get a handle on things first."

Florence set a goal to get rid of her $9,000 credit-card debt within six months. She made two very conscious, specific decisions: There would be no personal travel expenses for the next six months and she'd no longer lend money to friends. Both of these choices would be difficult for her, since she loved to travel and found it hard to say no to the people close to her. But Florence was in love with Russell and felt she had found her soul mate, so there was strong motivation to stick to the plan. She also changed other financial behaviors. Florence cut her impulse spending to a minimum, began making her loan payments on time, and applied unexpected money from bonuses and monetary gifts directly to her debt.

I also recommended Florence explore exchanging her luxury car for a more moderately priced one. She really loved driving her Mercedes and was reluctant to accept that suggestion, but she did look into having her bank refinance the car at a lower interest rate. Unfortunately, because of her poor credit history, the bank declined the request. This decline became another highly motivating factor for Florence, since she didn't want Russell to know that her credit report was not clean or be humiliated if her credit history affected their future purchases.

It's been only three months, but Florence's credit-card debt is down to $5,000 and she's feeling very proud of herself. She's also gotten a part-time job on weekends that could pay as much as $500 per day, so she should have no problem reaching her goal. "At first it felt overwhelming to think about getting rid of all of my debt. But now that I'm close to paying off the credit cards, I know I can use the same strategy to work on the other debts one by one. That way my new life with Russell won't be weighed down by my financial baggage."

Money troubles are one of the leading causes of divorce in this country, so by working to get her finances in order, Florence can help to give her upcoming marriage a better than average chance of success. Her new healthy money habits will give her and Russell an even greater opportunity for financial harmony and marital bliss. That certainly speaks to her heart, don't you think?

Without goals we tend to feel adrift—moving through life unmotivated and without purpose. Because you are reading this book, you obviously have a desire to gain financial control and get your money straight. And naturally, most people want to become debt free. That's certainly what I wanted for many years. I was clearly motivated because of how stressful and painful it had been carrying my debt for so long. But simply wanting to get rid of the debt didn't keep me as disciplined as I needed to be. After paying off $40,000 of the $50,000 worth of debt accumulated during my marriage, I found the last $10,000 incredibly difficult to get rid of. Until I started thinking about writing this book and became determined to be debt free long before its publication, I didn't have enough motivation to make it happen. Only after finding that particular burning desire and determining the reason *why* I needed to be debt free was I able to make my goal a reality.

Christine, a thirty-two-year-old high school teacher, loved her work. Nothing was more gratifying than imparting knowledge to young people and encouraging their dreams. Because her salary afforded her a comfortable lifestyle Christine had never been concerned about her finances or her debt. She was current on all of her bills and never felt the need to balance her checkbook. She had no emergency savings fund but wasn't concerned, because after all, she had good credit and plenty of it.

In her head, Christine estimated that she owed about $13,000 in credit-card debt—not too excessive, she felt, considering that her net income averaged about $3,000 per month. But Christine got the shock of her life when she applied for a debt consolidation loan and was turned down. Her debts had actually grown to $22,570 in just three years! How could this have happened? In looking back on her behavior, she realized she had used her credit cards for eating out, gasoline, travel, books, electronics, therapy, and three months' living expenses while between jobs.

Like many others, Christine had grown accustomed to living a lifestyle beyond her means. But deep in her heart, she had a vision of another life she wanted to lead. For years, she had dreamed of enrolling in a program through a well-known national organization that would allow her to teach in a rural community in Africa. She had recently started gathering information about the process and learned that it required a two-year commitment. But the next session of the program started the following year, and she wanted to eliminate her debts and get her life in order in only twelve months.

When Christine first became my client, I felt this was an ambitious objective. However, I can vividly remember her telephone call one year later, saying, "Glinda, thank you so much. I just wrote the last check. I'm now debt free and leaving in ten days." What an accomplishment for Christine! When asked what she felt made the difference in her ability to surmount the incredible obstacle, Christine stated three things. One: She had a goal. Being motivated by this tremendous opportunity and eagerly looking forward to it helped her tolerate a second job of teaching adult education classes at night to increase her income. Two: She had a tool. My book, *The Basic Money Management Workbook,* helped her to see what she was spending money on and where to cut. She also recognized some compulsive patterns. For instance, she frequently purchased things on credit cards even when she had cash in her pocket. This prompted her to stop and think, "Do I really need to buy this now?" and "Can I pay cash for it?" Finally, she had support. With my encouragement, guidance, and direction, she remained clear on her objectives. The financial counseling process made her be accountable to someone other than herself. And she needed that.

Christine kept it simple. She had a goal, a tool or methodology, and support. Most important, being extremely motivated by her goal provided the drive that was necessary to keep going even through the tough times. Christine is just one of many satisfied souls who used the passion and enthusiasm of their goal to accomplish their heart's desire.

What's your immediate motivation to get your financial house in order? What are your short-term goals? How about long-term? What do you keep postponing because you don't have the money? Maybe it's purchasing a new home so that each of your kids can have their own bedroom; or taking a Caribbean vacation for your mental health and being served margaritas by the pool; or how about starting an investment portfolio so you can take advantage of the booming stock market. Whatever creates a burning desire and motivates you to remain disciplined is the perfect goal for you.

Query 2: Do You Keep Your Goal Visible Throughout the Day and Formulate Action Steps to Achieve It?

Soon after Dr. Dennis Kimbro published his national bestseller, *Think and Grow Rich: A Black Choice,* I had an opportunity to hear him speak. I remember being entertained by his speech and impressed with him personally. He was very down-to-earth, easy to relate to, and had a great story full of challenging life experiences. With determination and perseverance, he overcame his obstacles, and his eventual success provided a basis for the strategies he shared with us that day. But I recall leaving the auditorium, saying to myself, "That was great, but he really didn't say anything I didn't already know. Every day I teach those same principles to my clients."

The next day I looked back over the few notes I had scribbled down on the seminar program and was reminded of two points that he made regarding goals. First, he had asked, "When you wake up in the morning and open your eyes, do you see your goals? If I were to go to your home and look in the mirror over the sink where you brush your teeth, would I see your goals? If I were to drive your car, would I see your goals? If I were to sit behind the desk where you spend eight to ten hours a day, would I see your goals?" Second, he said, "If you haven't achieved your goals yet, it's probably because they aren't clearly defined and visible." Obviously, this thought struck me at the time he said it, otherwise I wouldn't have written it down. But it really struck me as I reread it the next day. I thought, "Gee, goals are a key part of my financial program, and we always put them in writing. But even *my* goals are written in a notebook and are only occasionally looked at. Maybe I should make them more visible."

We all need to clarify our goals and make them visible for consistent reinforcement. Following that seminar, I took a large poster board and created the Goal Worksheet that is described in detail at the end of this chapter. After completing the chart, I placed it on my bedroom wall, where it was the first thing I'd see in the morning. Over the next couple of days, I became increasingly goal driven, and I started taking the action steps I had outlined on the chart. I made some telephone calls and was amazed at how quickly things started to happen in my business. By day three, phone calls were coming in with opportunities that weren't even directly related to the calls I had made but were nonetheless things I wanted to do to grow my business. One of the incoming calls resulted in my first national appearance on a television talk show! By getting clear on my goals, putting them in writing and taking action, I had demonstrated to the universe that I was ready for some things to happen, and the universe responded appropriately.

Having a clear vision of what you want is critical, but it is not the end-all solution to making your dreams come true. My new client, Renita, is great at defining and describing her goals. She's so good, she could teach a class on it. What Renita desires right now is a new home for herself and her three children. "I know exactly what I want," she says emphatically. "It's in writing and I even have a sacred space in my bedroom where I pray, meditate, and have a picture posted of my ideal house." Renita also carries the following description of the house in her daily planner:

"My right and perfect home is in Oakland, in or near a nature-filled area, a safe, well maintained, nontoxic, appreciating neighborhood; easy public and freeway transportation access, on quiet, nonthorough-fare street; structurally sound with solid foundation, good roof and floors; skylight, 4 plus bedrooms, 2½ bathrooms with windows, living room, den, basement, dining area, large closets and ample storage, upgraded kitchen and bath; large, low-maintenance backyard, fenced or private, garage, fireplace, space to develop structure and/or yard. Plus a cooperative, amenable seller willing to assist me as the buyer. Conscientious neighbors. Monthly mortgage not to exceed $900 per month."

That's pretty darn clear, isn't it? Renita admitted she thought it was a bit idealistic but not impossible. She and her children had been living in an apartment hoping to save enough money to buy her dream home. Things have always been tight for Renita financially, but she saves a little money each month and has a small amount set aside for a down payment. She has provided a full life for herself and her boys and has managed to stay out of debt in the process. She makes enough income to qualify for a home. But not the home she wants. And now, as her three boys get bigger, her family has started to outgrow the apartment, and the sense of urgency increases. After two years of visualizing and meditating on her dream house, she has yet to bring it into manifestation.

Renita has done the things Dr. Kimbro suggested—clearly defining her goal and making it visible. She has done what I suggested and determined the compelling reason she needs to move soon. She also has a solid spiritual practice of meditating on her goal regularly. But with all those things going for her, something important is still missing: Her goal is clearly visualized but her action steps aren't. Renita needs to take a closer look at what it will take to get from here to there and outline specific, detailed steps to take daily to begin to increase her income so she can qualify for her dream home.

To achieve your goals, you need to have clarity on what you want, why you want it, when you want it, and how to get it. Goals must be clearly defined and measurable. They must be specific but not rigid. They must also include target dates and have action steps so you know how to go about achieving them. For example, let's say your goal is to become debt free and the reason is that you want to move across the country and be close to your aging parents. If you relocate, you might need to take a job with less income. Carrying a $13,000 balance on your Visa card is very uncomfortable, so you set a target date of two years, intending to pay it off by January 1, 2003. Some of your action steps might be as follows: Stop charging on the card, get the lowest interest rates possible (in this case, let's say it's 8 percent), increase your monthly payments from $260 to $588 (the amount needed to pay off by January 1, 2003), and create monthly spending plans to factor in the new payment plus cash for all other expenses.

As a final step, make sure that at the end of each day you've done something to advance toward your objective. For example, did you take your lunch to work instead of eating out with coworkers? Did you resist the temptation to make an impulse purchase? Acknowledge all these small victories as stepping-stones to your ultimate success, and be sure to establish a daily ritual to visualize, affirm, and meditate on your goals.

As I mentioned before, after hearing Dr. Kimbro speak, I created my Goal Worksheet and began to take action. Because one of the goals on my chart was to be featured in *Black Enterprise*, one of my action steps was to do some networking and find out if anyone I knew was acquainted with someone at the magazine. I soon found out that no one was, so I took matters into my own hands. Sitting in my office one day, I decided to exercise my gut muscles. I reached for the current issue of *Black Enterprise*, located the telephone number, and called their New York office. I told the operator who I was and why I was calling. After being transferred a couple of times, I found myself speaking directly to the editor of the personal finance section. Again I explained who I was and why I was calling, and to my surprise he said, "Oh, we've been looking for some new resources on the West Coast. Fax me some information about yourself." I did immediately, and the following day I received my first assignment from *Black Enterprise*! Over the next twelve months, I appeared in the magazine four times and was even a featured speaker in 1999 at the Fourth Annual *Black Enterprise*/Bank of America Entrepreneurs Conference in Florida. A pretty good result from a couple of simple action steps!

I didn't know my relationship with *Black Enterprise* would evolve the way it did. One can never know these things. What I knew was if I got clear on what I wanted; if I put it down on paper, if I put it up where I could see it, if I drew upon the courage of gutsy black women past and present, if I walked through the fear, and if I checked in with myself each day to make sure I had made some effort toward my goal—that action would breed opportunity. And that was all I could ask for—an opportunity to share my gifts and reach my personal and professional goals in the process.

Query 3: Are You Directed Toward Achieving Balance in Your Life?

Vivian is one of my very best and oldest girlfriends. Maybe I should say she's a longtime friend, because she never hesitates to tell people that I'm the oldest—never mind it's by only four days. Vivian and I share a mutual admiration; she admires my professional accomplishments and I admire her personal accomplishments—she's been married to a wonderful man for ten years and is mother to three dogs and two cats. Vivian's incredibly devoted husband emotionally, spiritually, and financially supports, encourages, and champions every idea and every interest she's either imagined or endeavored. Granted, she has had great success in her life, such as going back to school at age forty-something to earn her undergraduate and graduate degrees, while I have had some incredibly wonderful personal relationships. But the degree to which each of us has become accomplished and achieved our success is based on the focus, energy, and priority we placed on our life goals—mine were professional and hers were personal.

To have a successful financial life, you can't focus just on your personal goals or your professional goals. Both areas need attention. And although it may seem counterintuitive, you can't focus just on making money. Even if you have lots of money, voids in other areas of your life will likely cause you to spend excessively—trying to fill the holes and alter the uncomfortable feelings—so the vicious cycle will continue. In order to be balanced and fulfilled, you must create and accomplish goals in all areas of your life.

In *One Day My Soul Just Opened Up*, author Iyanla Vanzant describes the word "balance" as "a state of being in proportion, one thing to another—to arrange so that one set of elements equals another." She goes on to say that balance in life means you should "Rest. Work. Play. Learn. Teach. Give. Receive. A little bit of this. A little bit of that. Stop. Go. Speak. Listen. Cry a little. Understand more. Pray a lot. Rejoice even more." So I like to further categorize goals using a simple format. As you are thinking about the life that you want, set personal goals in the following areas: financial, emotional, spiritual, intellectual, and physical. When you think about your professional goals, pinpoint them using the following categories: position, income, benefits, education, and location. You'll be surprised at how these different areas of your life can profoundly affect your financial well-being.

Query 4: Have You Established Appropriate Benchmarks to Judge Your Progress?

Back in 1981, while still an assistant manager in the banking industry and long before I had any inkling of starting the Bridgforth Financial Management Group, I happened to be interviewed for an article in *Black Enterprise* entitled "Ms. Money Manager." Although only age twenty-nine, I confidently chatted with the interviewer about my plans to retire by age forty-five. At the time, I was involved in the multilevel marketing company with my then husband and felt that it, not banking, would be my vehicle to the good life. My network marketing business associates and I had a strong desire for financial independence. But even with a good vehicle and our tremendous enthusiasm, it didn't happen. I realize now it was likely never going to happen because I had no strategic business plan, no specific action steps, and no benchmarks for interim assessment. I had just enthusiasm and dreams.

Naturally, everybody is different and individual goals and dreams necessitate different benchmarks. However, there are some general guidelines that all sisters can use to make sure they're on the road to a healthy financial life. Use the following financial benchmarks to assess what you've accomplished to date and pinpoint what you can strive for in the future:

In Your Twenties

- Work toward saving 10 percent of your income for all your future goals.
- Save up for vacations and major purchases in interest-bearing accounts instead of getting into the buy-now-pay-later habit, using credit cards.
- Don't be seduced into the "no payments and no interest for 12 months" selling techniques.
- Maintain an emergency fund of at least $500 in savings at all times.
- Start a 401K plan or IRA and make the maximum contribution allowable.
- Save for a down payment on a home.

In Your Thirties

- Keep no more than two credit-card accounts; pay off your balances every month.
- Build up your emergency fund to cover three to six months' living expenses.

- Make maximum contributions to a 401K or IRA.
- Buy a house, co-op, or condo; if you buy a house, consider a duplex for rental income.
- Start a mutual-fund account using dollar-cost averaging to your advantage. (Dollar-cost averaging is the principle that investing equal amounts each month earns more in the long run than investing a lump sum at the end of the year.)
- Meet with a financial planner to develop a long-range investment strategy for your retirement plan.
- Increase your knowledge about the stock market by joining an investment club.

In Your Forties

- Increase monthly investment contributions as your income grows and according to the long-term investment strategy you've worked out with a professional.
- Consider starting your own business; discuss opening a self-employed retirement plan such as a Keogh or Simplified Employee Pension plan with your financial adviser.
- Buy a home if you haven't already; open a home-equity line of credit for extraordinary expenses. (Unlike personal credit-card interest, home-equity-loan interest is usually tax deductible.)
- Buy real estate property you can rent to earn income.
- Investigate and purchase insurance for aging parents' long-term care.

In Your Fifties

- Decide when you want to retire and plan how you will enjoy your financial freedom.
- Meet with a financial adviser to review investment strategies and asset allocation: Decide when you want to switch emphasis from growing your assets to conserving them.
- If you're considering early retirement, you might want to pay off your mortgage first.

- If you continue to work and earn a high income for a number of years, you may want to keep your mortgage for the tax write-off.
- Investigate and purchase insurance for long-term care in your own old age.

In Your Sixties
- Explore options to retire or not.
- Manage cash flow to make sure retirement funds outlast retirement.
- Have fun and enjoy a new, exciting chapter in your book of life.

Use these financial benchmarks as a guide when you begin the "design your life" process of setting annual goals. Of course, you'll need to tailor some of these to your current situation and map out action steps to reach the different objectives. But consistently referring to these benchmarks will keep you moving forward. And after a lifetime of hard work, you'll be able to retire in comfort and style.

Query 5: Have You Established a Set of Spiritual Practices That Put You in Touch with Your Higher Self?

Because this financial program utilizes a holistic approach, it's important to develop a spiritual practice. These days, our hectic lifestyles rarely allow us time to slow down, quiet our minds, and go within to communicate with a Higher Power for financial guidance. Only when circumstances become dire and all resources are exhausted do we finally turn to a spiritual source for help with money problems. We're all probably guilty, at some point in our lives, of the well-intentioned proposition to God, "If you fix this problem for me this time, I promise I won't ever do it again."

Prayer and meditation should be used to complement our concrete financial plans and actions. A consistent spiritual practice allows you an opportunity to express gratitude for your blessings and maintain perspective on the "source" of goodness in your life and helps alleviate the onset of paralyzing fear, worry, and avoidance when financial challenges arise. The practice of prayer and meditation focuses the mind, eliminates distractions, and creates a sense of calmness and peace. During this state of repose, the way to satisfy our wants and needs usually becomes clear.

In his books, *Healing Words* and *Prayer Is Good Medicine*, author Larry Dossey, M.D., examines the scientific evidence of the healing power of prayer and effectively shows the connection between prayer and improved health. I agree with him and suggest that even an *attitude* of simple prayerfulness can set the stage for financial peace of mind by letting go of fear and worry and opening oneself to receive the natural goodness and abundance of life. Whether we call them "answered prayers" or "miracles," positive results can happen.

For example, while on disability, in the process of divorce and facing foreclosure, I sat on the floor of my transition apartment with a list of unpaid bills and no anticipated income to pay them. After several hours of excruciating worry, I used meditation to quiet my mind. Then I had a conversation with God about my precarious financial predicament. Holding the list of bills in hand, I said, "Look, God, this is what needs to be paid. I've done everything I know to do to deal with these bills, and I'm fresh out of ideas. You have to take care of them, because I don't know what else to do." Then I took a deep breath and let go. Twenty minutes later, the telephone rang and it was a relative who said, "Hi, Glinda, how are you? Do you need any money?" Three days later, a check arrived in the mail for enough money to cover the bills plus $500 extra!

Granted, this experience was pretty extraordinary, and simply putting yourself in the hands of God isn't going to balance your checkbook. We are all in control of our own financial destiny. But it does demonstrate the ways in which spiritual practices can open us to new insights, create new opportunities for tangible results, and bring comfort in times of stress, and ultimately, financial peace of mind.

Be Prepared for the Unexpected

Despite the best planning, life doesn't always unfold on schedule and the road to your goals may be bumpy. That's why it is vitally important, no matter what your financial straits or how badly you want to decrease your credit-card debt, to try to keep your life, medical, automobile, and property insurance policies paid up. A basic relationship may change, such as a parent's death or a decision by you or your mate to file for divorce. You or a family member may contract an unexpected illness. Your plant, company, or office may be sold, closed, or downsized, taking your job with it. A natural disaster like a tornado, hurricane, earthquake, fire, or flood may destroy your personal property or belongings. If, God forbid, something like that happens, put your regular routine on hold to cope with the situation at hand. Once life is back to normal, however, be sure to pick up your goals where you left off. Don't let an unexpected setback be an excuse to quit. If you get back on track and continue to strive toward your goals, you will soon be able to remember that downtime as a challenge you overcame. A few rocky patches on the road to success make ultimate victory all the sweeter.

Exercise One: Brainstorm Your Desires

To establish your goals and motivating reasons, let's brainstorm. Think about what makes you happy and lifts your spirit. It may or may not be material items. As you jot those things down on a piece of paper, don't worry about details or putting them in any order. We'll fine-tune and categorize them later. For now, think about what brings you joy and satisfies your soul. What are your needs in life? What are your wants?

Start with your body. Begin at the top of your head and work your way down. For instance, would you like a new hairstyle, eyeglasses, or dental work? What about your brain? Is it in need of stimulation? Perhaps you'd like to take a class or have time to read more books. Continue to work down the rest of your body and then move out to your environment. Would you make any changes in your living space? Move from room to room, adding to your list. Next, consider your family. What would you do regarding your family that would bring you joy and satisfaction? Spend a few minutes focusing on other areas like transportation, job, friends, and community. Keep this list handy and add to it when things come to mind that have gone undone for a while. Look for things that stir you, make your heart skip a beat, and make you want to sing for joy.

Exercise Two: Creating the Goal Worksheet

In this exercise, we'll be using the list you created by brainstorming your goals and desires. Start by going back over your list and separating the personal items from the professional ones. Then, on a separate sheet of paper with the heading Personal Goals, create five columns, using the following categories to further sort your goals: financial, emotional, spiritual, intellectual, and physical. Some items may overlap in different categories, but pick the one that feels most appropriate to you. Next, separate each item within the category into three columns: A, most important; B, important; and C, would be nice. Last, prioritize the items in each column. What's most important to your quality of life right now? What would you like to accomplish first? For example, my early financial category looked like this:

Personal Goals

Financial

Column A:
1. Cover basic necessities such as food, shelter, and clothing.
2. Meet monthly spending plan.
3. Eliminate financial crisis.

Column B:
1. Pay bills in a timely manner.
2. Become financially stable.
3. Obtain some wants, such as a massage each month.

Column C:
1. Take a trip.
2. Pay off debt.
3. Gain financial independence.

Use this as an example to sort each item on your brainstorming list. You may want to complete this exercise on your own first, then refine the list with your spouse or partner. Now take the professional goals from your brainstorming list and do the same thing. You might consider the following categories: position, income, education, benefits, and location. As an entrepreneur, your categories may be different. I set my professional goals in the various areas where I feel I can generate income or gain exposure. For example: clients, keynotes, seminars/workshops, books, tapes, corporate clients, magazines, television, and radio.

Now that you have your personal goals distinguished from your professional goals, appropriate categories determined for each of those areas, and goals listed that you'd like to accomplish in each category, take a deep breath! How does it feel? Have you covered all the areas that make up your complete self? Does it feel balanced? Are the goals clearly defined? We're not quite done yet. We have two more steps to complete this part of the process. Next, refer back to each of your goals and estimate a date by which you'd like to accomplish each one. Don't be afraid to commit to it in writing. Target dates are just that—a target to shoot for. You should be serious and realistic when you set them, but know that like goals, they are specific yet flexible.

Finally, just like Renita, you must establish the action steps that are crucial to achieving your goals. An example of the action steps Renita might take to position herself to qualify for her larger dream home is as follows:

Category: Income

Goal: Increase income 20 percent

Action: 1. Assess current qualifications and skill level.
2. Determine areas of interest.
3. Assess opportunities with current employer and others.
4. Talk to people they know in the industry of interest.
5. Schedule five informational interviews.
6. Apply for a new position at a higher salary.

Exercise Three: Make Your Goals Visible

Take some time and go through your favorite magazines looking for pictures of things that symbolize the goals you identified for each category in Exercise 2. Look for colorful photographs that catch your eye. For example, if you decided under the emotional category that a Caribbean vacation with your mate is your desire, look for photographs of a happy couple holding hands and strolling along a white sand beach with tropical blue water rushing over their ankles. Or if under financial you'd like a $10,000 raise in annual salary—as another resource—visit a toy store and purchase some play money. Try to find the kind that looks like real currency. Get $50 and $100 bills if you can—I always find them to be more motivational.

Next, take a poster board and draw a large circle similar to a pie chart, dividing it equally into the number of categories you are working on. Now label each section outside the circle with the goal category and paste your pictures in the appropriate section. At a glance, you should be able to see at least one image for each of your goals on this chart.

I recommend you place the poster where you can see it frequently or in a place where you can view it during your most private moments. One year I placed mine behind my bedroom door, since most times if I were in the bedroom, the door would be closed. This way, I was sure to focus on it when I was in a restful state—first thing in the morning and last thing at night. This helped me reinforce and manifest the dreams that speak to my heart.

Exercise Four: Create an Altar of Abundance

An altar is a sacred space where you can get quiet and focus your attention on making a spiritual connection with the Divine. Create such a space in your home for prayer, meditation, to express gratitude, and to focus on the prosperous lifestyle of your dreams. "An altar provides a focal point," says Harriet Y. Wright, a Bay Area consultant who has designed public event altars for organizations as well as personal altars for individuals. She goes on to say: "It gathers and grounds spiritual energy that can lead to clarity and conscious action. Thus, an altar helps move your intentions and goals from abstract to the visual and visceral."

In my own experience with an altar ritual, I was quite pleased with the results. Earlier this year, I was feeling overwhelmed and out of sorts largely because of having several important projects going on at once. I was physically tired and mentally restless at the same time. So I created an altar whose purpose was to help bring peace into my life. With the guidance of Ms. Wright, I gathered items that symbolized the feelings I wanted to manifest. I kept it simple and selected the following items:

1. A small heart-shaped potpourri container
2. An old black-and-white photograph of myself at age three with my best friend, Jackie, who was age four
3. A small bowl of water with a fresh gardenia floating in it
4. A light-blue scented candle with various seashells at the bottom
5. A small statue of an angel

Next, I picked a corner of my bedroom and placed each item on a small table. For at least fifteen minutes each morning and fifteen minutes each evening, I would sit at the altar, close my eyes, and consciously focus on one item at a time. My meditation went as follows: "Holy Spirit, God Almighty. Thank you for this day and for all of your Creation. Open my heart to give love and to receive love from others. Fill my heart with self-love and surround my inner child with joy. Thank you for the beauty of nature and the tranquillity of the ocean, as I know that beauty and tranquillity are in me. May the angels continue to guide and protect me as I move forward along my spiritual path." Using this ritual, within two days I was again centered and at peace with myself.

To create your altar of abundance, select items that symbolize prosperity, wealth, and bounty. As an example, Ms. Wright suggests that a horn of plenty filled with colorful fruits, a fertility doll, or a collection of gold coins or fine gems can focus your energy on financial increase. There is no special way that an altar is *supposed* to look. It takes on the character of its creator and evolves over time. Keep in mind, this exercise is not to encourage your viewing money as a "god" or beginning to worship material objects. Instead, it's about creating a physical manifestation of your goals so that you can be reminded of them on a regular basis.

 *Chapter Five*

Prescription 2:
Balance Your Checkbook
and Know Your Net Worth

I love receiving updates from former clients on how their lives have changed since financial counseling. It's what makes the job well worth it. I received the following e-mail on July 31, 1998:

"Guess what? I made my LAST credit-card payment on June 1. I AM NOW DEBT FREE!! It feels wonderful, but it still has not quite sunk in yet. Thank you, thank you, thank you! I could never have done it without your help and guidance. I can still remember the first day I walked into your office, November 9, 1995. My head was spinning when I left. I had so many action steps to take! Thank God, I did every single one. I was $11,000 in debt; now I have almost $11,000 in savings. The money I was paying toward my credit-card debt will now go into my savings. I am still tracking my daily and monthly spending, and my checkbook is balanced every month without fail! I even went to Aruba in April (had a fabulous time). Everything was paid for in full when I received the bill in May. I had paid for my plane tickets back in December. What a great feeling to be in control of my finances!"

This enthusiastic note is from Rachel, a thirty-eight-year-old technical writer who had been struggling financially for years—juggling bills and living paycheck to paycheck. This sister knew she was spending more money monthly than was coming in but was too afraid to face it. She refused to use a check register to account for checks written and felt some degree of checkbook security by having overdraft coverage on her account. But her mounting debt of $11,000 prompted her to seek financial counseling.

With my help, Rachel discovered that most of her debt had resulted from automatic credit-card advances to her checking account for overdraft protection. She had never looked closely at her monthly credit-card bills and, amazingly, had a shopping bag with over fifteen years' worth of unopened checking account statements! Had Rachel opened her mail, she would have known the advances to her checking account sometimes totaled $300 to $400 per month. Over time, they had spiraled out of control because of her fear of dealing with not only her bank statements and the basic paperwork but with the emotions at the root of her excess spending.

Rachel was a brown-skinned woman with long, thick hair that extended below her shoulders. When she walked past, brothers' heads would do a 180-degree turn and sisters would wonder, "Is that her real hair or a weave?" But even though she was very attractive, Rachel didn't feel good about herself because of her financial Achilles' heel. In our discussions, she acknowledged that she dated regularly, and when in a romantic relationship, something was fulfilled within her and she hardly ever went to the store. However, if there was no intimacy or affection in her life, she had a tendency to go shopping. Rachel used different means to take care of herself and nurture her self-esteem, such as getting her hair done weekly. Her mother had always said, "You can have on the best-looking outfit, but if your hair doesn't look good, it won't matter." So Rachel stayed committed to her standing hair appointment even though she couldn't really afford $25 each week. Eventually, because of the state of her finances, she started to feel extremely guilty about this extravagance, and about spending money on entertainment.

But in addition to guilt over her uncontrolled spending, there was something more going on with Rachel. She was consumed with fear and anxiety that seemed to go beyond her $11,000 debt. Halfway through our first session together, Rachel admitted that her checking account had an unexplained payroll deposit of $13,000 that had been sitting there for two weeks. She knew the money didn't belong to her, but because she was tight on funds that month, she had used over $300 of this money. Rachel hoped this windfall was the miracle she had been praying for, but she also knew in her heart of hearts that the error would eventually be discovered and she'd have to repay the money she had used. This additional checkbook worry had pushed her over the edge and driven her to seek support. My first recommendation was that Rachel come clean and report the error so she could immediately alleviate a major part of her anxiety. Next, we began forming the steps to stabilize her spending and get control of her finances.

The checkbook was the main financial tool that Rachel used, yet it had her—a mature and well-educated black woman—terrified. Believe it or not, for some African American adults, a checking account is met with an extreme amount of reservation. Depending on the generation and socioeconomic status of the individual, checking accounts may have never been a part of their life experience. In generations past, African Americans with limited education and limited resources feared the complexity of checking accounts and resorted early on to using money orders and paying cash. Other blacks may have had a checkbook in the past but become so frustrated with trying to maintain it properly that they gave up. Some black folks have had banks give up on them—after chronic overdrafts their accounts were closed by the bank. If that happened and the account was closed with an overdrawn balance or bad checks still in circulation, the person was likely reported to an agency such as ChexSystem or Telecheck, which maintain negative records of checking accounts much as credit bureaus do with credit-card accounts.

Having a record with one of these companies is sufficient reason for a bank to decline a request to open a new account (checking or savings), so blacks are often forced to use check-cashing companies that charge exorbitant fees. For example, the fee for cashing most checks is 2 percent on checks up to $2,000 and 3 percent for checks over $2,000. So if you cashed a check for $800, you would pay a $16 fee. And if you needed to cash a check for $2,500, you would pay a whopping $75 fee! Another reason blacks are compelled to use these expensive facilities is that banks have systematically moved out of black communities, claiming insufficient profit margins. If blacks choose to travel to other neighborhoods to do their banking, the new banks are leery because they are from outside the area. So we're often caught between the proverbial rock and a hard place, and our options have been extremely limited.

Nevertheless, by following the 7 Prescriptions, especially Prescription 2, Rachel was able to correct her dysfunctional financial and checkbook habits over time. And taking a look at your own checking account is the second step toward an abundant and prosperous lifestyle.

Eliminate Checkbook Chaos

Regardless of a person's ethnicity, poor checkbook habits are very common and are often the place where financial chaos starts. Because the checkbook is a tool that most of us use on a daily basis, we have lots of opportunity to sabotage it. Usually we are afraid to maintain it properly because we don't want to know how little money we have. Sometimes we may just say "Why bother with the checkbook, since it probably won't balance to the bank statement anyway." It's a frustrating experience and hard on the ego when we see ourselves as intelligent black women who can't seem to master a simple checking account. Some of us go into denial by sticking our heads in the sand, hoping the account will balance itself. Or we try to fool ourselves by saying it's not that bad or that important. Others, like Rachel, become paralyzed and avoid dealing with a checking account by storing their bank statements without even opening the envelope.

These behaviors, although they help us get by temporarily, ultimately lead to vagueness and uncertainty where our checking accounts are concerned—and that fogginess leads to unnecessary fear and anxiety with every aspect of our money. These unsettling emotions can also translate into a mind-set of scarcity and lack that further contributes to the overall unhealthy state of our finances.

It's of vital importance to balance your checking account monthly by walking step by step through the reconciliation process. Some sisters try to use shortcuts—like calling the bank every other day to see which checks have cleared. Or checking their balance and last five transactions for free by accessing their account through an ATM. At least, that's doing something to monitor your account. But it's an unnecessary, time-consuming step. (Plus, at some banks you're charged for each telephone call over a specified number.)

If you follow the day-to-day healthy checkbook habits presented here, it should be necessary to reconcile or balance your account only once a month. In addition to the confidence you'll get by knowing how much money you have at all times, it's the best way to ensure there's been no accounting or mathematical errors on either your part or the bank's. And banks do make mistakes. For example, one day a new client described a letter she had received from her bank. "Dear Ms. Smith," the letter said. "We are sorry that the deposit you made to your account on May 15 for $600 was not credited until September 7. We apologize for any inconvenience this may have caused you." And wouldn't you know, my client had no idea the deposit was ever missing!

Knowing that you have control over your checkbook is very empowering. The joy and exaltation that clients display the first time they balance their checkbook is fun to watch. The instant my client Jasmine hit the calculator button and realized the $597.38 in her checkbook register equaled the $597.38 on the bank statement worksheet, she leaped out of her chair and began dancing around my office! The thirty-three-year-old prim and proper librarian could not have been more thrilled. But neither of us realized the extent of her shift in consciousness that day. Jasmine later became so skilled at using Quicken (the personal finance software program that organizes finances) that she'd take great pride in bringing all sorts of graphs and pie charts to our sessions to demonstrate her monthly financial progress.

Just like Jasmine, you, too, can experience financial jubilation. So let's begin by healing your unhealthy checkbook.

Helpful Hints for Checkbook Management

Several years before starting my own business, I hired Jessica, a graphic designer, to typeset my self-published book, *The Basic Money Management Workbook*. I provided her with the manuscript, and a week later she returned the completed project to me. At that time, Jessica indicated how working on my project had been a blessing to her. While working on one of the sections, also called "Helpful Hints for Checkbook Management," she read the tip *Deduct automatic payments and service charges,* which prompted her to take a close look at her own checking account statement. "To my surprise, I discovered the health club membership that I canceled twelve months ago was still being deducted from my account. And because I never balance my checkbook, the oversight had gone unnoticed for a whole year." Had Jessica known about the Helpful Hints, she would have caught the problem earlier. Once aware of the error, Jessica contacted the health club, which verified its records and promptly reimbursed her the $600 in membership fees! As luck would have it, Jessica not only made money from typesetting, she got an unexpected $600 to boot.

To achieve mastery over our checkbooks, we must become vigilant in maintaining checkbook records. Dedication to the small daily activities will make the difference between success and failure. It's important to stop manipulating money and demonstrate a willingness to improve our checkbook habits. The following are some helpful hints to keep your checkbook straight and maintain a friendly relationship with it. Pay close attention to each item listed below and be honest with yourself if you are guilty of any unhealthy practices.

Use a register consistently to list checks and deposits. I can hear some of you already: "But I use duplicate checks, so I don't need to use a register." Yes, you do! Duplicate checks are good in that you have a carbon copy of what you've written. But few people use the space provided on the copy to bring account balances forward. Also, if you ever do ATM transactions or debit-card purchases, listing them on the carbon copy is nearly impossible because of the small space provided; therefore you can't be sure of your balance at any given time. So each time you make a transaction—be it writing a check, an ATM withdrawal, or a deposit—use the register that's included in each new box of printed checks to record what you've done. If you don't have one, ask for one at your bank. It's free of charge and a key checkbook tool. Also, keep your register in close proximity to your checks. Use the checkbook cover provided with your initial order, or, if you're using a wallet, make sure it's clutter free so that it easily accommodates both your checks and your register. That way, when you write your check, there's no excuse. You'll see the register and promptly use it. Finally, if you use Quicken—even though it balances your checkbook, pays your bills, and creates reports and graphs—don't depend on the software check register that automatically updates when you input your checks. Chances are you're not carrying your computer around in your purse, so there's likely to be some level of vagueness about your balance while out spending if you don't use a manual checkbook register. I highly recommend Quicken because it is inexpensive—a basic program costs about $34.95—and it's an easy way to keep your finances organized. But to start out, I feel the manual system is an invaluable way to fully understand the process.

List checks immediately in your register and deduct the amount from your balance. Don't allow yourself to be rushed at store checkout counters. Fill out as much of your check and check register as you can while your items are being rung up and then complete your record-keeping after you get the total. Don't use Post-it notes or jot things down in a daily planner. Take your time and write entries clearly and carefully in the register itself. Use a pencil so you can erase if necessary and avoid making messy scratch-outs with a pen. Be sure to carry your balance forward immediately. People behind you in line can wait ten seconds more while you take this necessary step. Also, always use exact amounts in your register—no rounding up. Don't play the game with yourself that a few cents here and there creates a cushion in the account. It doesn't promote clarity with money, and what's more, you'll never be able to balance your checkbook accurately.

Don't write postdated checks. Writing postdated checks—checks with a date at some time in the future—is just another way of creating debt. You're receiving merchandise or service today for payment in the future. It's a very easy way to get yourself overextended, and you'll again be playing financial catch-up. When you write postdated checks, you give up control of your checking account. According to my banker, "Technically, the check becomes legal tender and is cashable once you write it, regardless of the date. The only exception is if it specifically states, 'Do not cash before (specific date).' In other words, if the check is deposited early and gets past the teller, it could get through the system without anyone noticing the date and cause your account to be overdrawn. Also, don't write checks before depositing funds to cover them. This practice is called "kiting," and it is illegal. There's no need to create unnecessary drama in your life by having to race to the bank to make last-minute deposits to avoid expensive overdraft charges.

Deduct automatic payments and service charges. Insurance companies and health clubs often use automatic payment processing as a convenience for you and for them. But forgetting to make the deduction from your account can be a problem. If you can't live without automatic deductions, be sure to deduct charges on the first of the month so you don't forget. If you have an interest-bearing checking account, record any interest added to your account when you receive your statement. Also, document as much information as you can in your register when you write checks, such as dates covering subscriptions, dues, or service bills that come other than monthly. That makes it easy to trace and determine when the next payment is due. Know what kind of service-charge plan you have on your account. What's your monthly fee? Are you charged to use the debit card? Is there a cost for telephone calls to the customer service center? Be aware of what's being deducted from your account; otherwise, you'll have difficulty getting the numbers to add up.

Avoid ATM card purchases or point-of-sale transactions if you are not disciplined enough to write them down at the time of the purchase. Because the receipts for these purchases look much like cash receipts, they can easily be discarded before deducting them from your checkbook. If a transaction is done as a Visa check card as opposed to an ATM transaction, you'll need to sign the receipt. But again, it's still easy to get confused and skip deducting the amount from your balance. Forgetting to write down one or two point-of-sale transactions can easily cause you to become overdrawn, especially if you have limited funds in your account and you're not careful. Also, minimize your visits to the ATM. If you make lots of withdrawals for $20, they all start to look alike after a while and you may not be able to account for them accurately.

Don't use the overdraft-coverage feature as a crutch to ensure that none of your checks bounce. Instead, properly manage your checking account and there won't be any need to worry about becoming overdrawn and causing debt or expensive fees to accumulate. If you have compulsive spending patterns, you absolutely must delete your overdraft coverage. It's very easy to play games with yourself using this feature to create debt—remember Rachel's problem. Furthermore, if you are $10 overdrawn, the bank could transfer in $50 increments from your credit card (plus charge $4 for each transfer). Not only are you paying this fee, your interest rate on the advance is probably 18 to 20 percent and you'll spend the extra $40 that might not have been used otherwise. If you use a line of credit to cover overdrafts, your bank may transfer the exact amount needed, but watch your money mind-set. It's easy to start thinking of this available credit as additional cash in the account when it's not really cash—it's a liability once you spend it, and it adds up.

Balance your checkbook as soon as your statement is received and report any errors immediately to the bank. If no errors are reported within fourteen days (some banks allow up to sixty days), the bank assumes all checks are genuine. As for electronic transfer errors, they must be reported within sixty days. If you question a transaction and it takes the bank more than ten days to investigate, they'll often temporarily credit your account until the investigation is complete. Remember, faithfully reconciling your account each month gives you tremendous confidence and control when you know your account is balanced to the penny. You also eliminate the nagging worry, *Do I have enough money to cover this check?* Most statements arrive at the same time every month, so if you need an extra nudge, mark it in your day planner.

If you're part of a couple, maintain separate accounts—yours, mine, and ours. The checkbook can be a source of conflict for many couples. Problems tend to occur when one partner is less than diligent in record keeping or when a person feels controlled and restricted at having to account to the other for every dollar spent. I usually recommend keeping three checking accounts—a household account to cover family bills and two separate personal accounts to satisfy each person's need for autonomy. Your paycheck should go into your personal account, and then you and your partner can both transfer a certain amount of funds into the household account each month. Both partners should be aware of what's happening with the household account, but only one need write out checks to pay household expenses. Clarification should be made in advance with your partner to determine what expenses are paid for from personal checking accounts, such as lunches, hair care, manicures, massages, and so on.

Prereconcilement

Balancing your checkbook can be an overwhelming, anxiety-provoking activity. It can also be a pleasurable experience—one that affirms you as a financially responsible adult. I met a sister at a Colorado conference who described the ritual she went through each month when she sat down to reconcile her account. "I take out my checkbook, my bank statement, and then a bottle of wine. I take a drink and usually follow up by lighting a candle, then some aromatherapy and a little meditation." I chuckled when she told me this. This sister was definitely on the right track as far as being in a relaxed state of mind. Calming your nerves is a good thing, but I also want you to be clearheaded when you get started. So follow her meditation ritual if you're overanxious, but let's save the champagne for the postreconcilement celebration!

Don't make balancing your checkbook out to be more than it is. You don't need to know algebra or complex calculus formulas. The concept is simple. <u>How much money did you start the month with?</u> <u>What did you add? And what did you subtract?</u> If you can deal with this basic arithmetic, you can balance your checkbook. Schedule a specific time when you can focus without interruption on your checkbook. Then repeat this affirmation three times with enthusiasm and gusto: <u>*I am a financially responsible adult and I can DO this!*</u>

Reconcilement

To balance your checkbook, you simply want to reconcile your records to the bank's records. Keep in mind, everything that actually happens within your account is reflected on the checking account statement— either in the section "Deposits and credits" or "Withdrawals and debits." Begin by going over your statement and matching it against your register. Place a check mark by every transaction listed in the register that corresponds correctly with the statement. Now is the time to add any fees or interest payments to your register that you may have overlooked. Once you account for all these items in your check register, there should be no problem in balancing your account.

Next, we want to deal with any outstanding payments or checks to bring the ending balance on the statement right up-to-date. On the back of your statement is a worksheet to help you do this. Some of you may have never noticed this document before. Although it can look intimidating and complex, it really involves only five simple steps:

Ending balance shown on the statement	_____
Add any deposits you've made not shown on the statement	+ _____
Subtotal	_____
Subtract outstanding checks and debits	- _____
Equals your ending balance	_____

The ending balance should agree—to the penny—with the balance in your check register. If it's off by ten cents, your account is out of balance. Now, it's not necessary for you to be obsessive and spend five hours looking for a ten-cent error, but I would go through the steps once more to verify you used the correct numbers. If you still come up with a difference, and it's a nominal amount, you can take the bank's ending balance as your own this time. Don't berate yourself because it didn't balance exactly. Instead, acknowledge and commend yourself for the new behavior—tracking and keeping records. Focus on being more accurate in the future. If balancing problems persist or if the difference is more than a nominal amount, use the following steps to find your error and account for the difference. Be aware that it could also be a combination of small errors.

The Most Common Checkbook Errors

- Make sure you deducted all charges, fees, and withdrawals shown on your statement (but not in your check register) that may apply to your account. Also, be sure to add any dividends or any deposits shown on your statement (but not in your check register) that apply to your account.

- If the amount of your difference is divisible by the number 9, your error could be a transposition. For example, if your check was for $63 and you wrote $36 in your register, the difference is $27, which is divisible by 9. So carefully verify your numbers again.

- Make sure you have not inadvertently listed a deposit in the check column or a check in the deposit column. It sounds a little strange, but I've done it on more than one occasion. Sometimes we are in such haste and so distracted that we're unaware of making such an obvious error.

- Check for microencoding errors (the encoded check amount in the lower right-hand corner of your canceled check). When checks are processed at the bank, they go through a "proof of deposit" system, meaning an operator manually inputs the amount of your check and balances it to the deposit of the person or entity receiving credit. If you wrote a check for $50 and they accidentally added an extra 0, your check would be processed as $500. Normally, this type of error is caught right away because the operator's work would be out of balance. But it's not impossible for it to slip by, so you should eliminate that option as the cause of your error.

If You're Balancing Your Checkbook After a Period of Neglect

If it's been months or even years since you balanced your account, you don't have to go back to the beginning and work your way forward. But you'll have to assume the bank has been correct up to this point. Let's go through the steps to determine the correct balance for you to begin using, then you can balance to the bank statement the next month:

1. Call the bank for an account balance and all checks paid since the last statement.
2. Update your check register, indicating which checks have been paid.
3. Identify all outstanding checks and total the amount.
4. Deduct the outstanding checks from the bank's balance. Use the remaining amount as your new balance forward.
5. Record all future transactions and balance to next month's statement so you no longer have to take the bank's word for it.

You Did It!

So there you have it. Contrary to your former belief, you don't need to be a rocket scientist to balance your checkbook. Now's the time to open that bottle of wine. As you go forward, just follow these suggestions and be aware there are many little things you can be charged for. For instance, most of us know we're charged $1.50 for ATM transactions done at banks other than our own, or $18 to $25 for overdrafts. But did you know it may be costing you $1.50 to speak to a customer service representative by phone; 25 cents for point-of-sale purchases using your ATM card or ATM check card; or $2 per month for including canceled checks in the statement the bank mails to you each month? And some banks will even charge you if you don't maintain a high enough balance. If you haven't already, ask for and read your bank's Account and Service Fee brochure and its Checking Account Disclosure brochure. They're very informative and can be very illuminating too. That way you'll know where any little fees are coming from and possibly avoid them—these little amounts add up fast.

I recommend using the manual balancing system described above for a minimum of three to six months. It will help you reestablish a connection with your money. The time and attention you give to your finances in this way—taking pencil to paper—helps to make your finances less mysterious and remote. Later you can move to a software program like Quicken that maintains your checkbook register, reconciles your account quickly, and provides other features such as financial reports, categorizing expenses, budgeting, and easy tax record keeping. But for now, unless you're extremely comfortable with a computer, it can keep you a bit too detached from your money. Besides, many people who use Quicken as the checkbook register update their records only once or twice per month, and that's not enough for someone who needs to get her money straight. It's much easier and much more effective to do it as you go, payment by payment.

After two or three months of diligently following the Helpful Hints and reconcilement steps, if you are still not balancing your checkbook properly, think about what could be sabotaging your success. Consider your belief system and any negative self-talk. Do you say to yourself, "I'll never balance my account," "I'm hopeless and stupid," or "I'm not smart enough." Even if you say these things in jest, they imprint on your subconscious mind and you start to believe them. So make it a habit to stop yourself immediately by saying, "Oh, no—don't go there! I'm a powerful sister with a brilliant mind, and I can do this!"

Online Banking

Black women are now computer savvy and can navigate easily through cyberspace. Thus, more and more of us do online banking. This is great—it means we can do the following types of services at any time, day or night, seven days a week: access our primary checking account for information and up-to-date lists of transactions; check balances and transfer funds electronically among the accounts that we own; pay most bills; and obtain bank product and service information.

Payments and transfers can be done in three different ways: Transactions designated as "Today" are done immediately if completed by a certain cut-off time, usually around three-thirty P.M. Otherwise, they are completed the following business day. Transactions designated as "Future" can be done up to 364 days in advance. For example, if today is February 5, you can schedule a payment or transfer to automatically be made on May 20 of the same year. Finally, a "Recurring" transaction is one you request be made in the same amount to the same payee or account on a specified regular basis (e.g., weekly, biweekly, monthly). So let's say that to make sure you build your savings account, you choose not to wait until the end of the month to see how much money is left over to save. (We know how poorly that works, don't we?) You can decide to become proactive and set up a recurring payment of $100 on the fifteenth of each month to be deducted from your checking account and credited to your savings account. This way you've made a wonderful financial commitment to yourself—but you need to make sure the $100 is in your checking on the fifteenth. Otherwise you'll be overdrawn. But ideally, we've already established healthy checkbook habits and know how to avoid that kind of drama.

Determine Your Net Worth

Another critical step in cultivating financial savvy and power is being clear on the difference between your self-worth and your net worth. Simply put, if all your assets were liquidated and your debts paid off, what amount would be left? Is that amount your value or worth as a human being? Of course not, no matter what the figure is. But unfortunately, many of us have bought into a societal notion that associates the value of a human being with their equity—the greater the dollar amount, the greater the person's worth.

Black women are no exception to the old masculine way of thinking—he (or she) who makes the most and has the most wins. I even find myself on occasion comparing my financial status with others'—especially people with high corporate incomes, stock options, luxury homes, and fancy cars. What's insane about this habit is that I love my life today and I know that I'm exactly where I'm supposed to be right now. I love my work, the money and benefits, the rhythm of my life, and especially my freedom. I know very well that comparing myself with others is the fastest way to diminish my self-esteem. When I catch myself thinking this way, I quickly remind myself of my path, my plan, Divine timing, and that the numbers don't mean as much as the quality of my life. Then I take a few deep breaths and get grounded again.

Although my intention in writing this book is to help you get your money straight and increase your net worth by sharing strategies and the fundamental skills necessary to make it happen, it's important to always remember: You are not your net worth. That dollar amount has nothing to do with the really important things—how you live your life with integrity, show love to your family, communicate with brothers and sisters, and help them up the ladder of success. When you genuinely love yourself, you easily give and receive joy. Your worth increases immeasurably when you take an afternoon and volunteer to read stories to schoolchildren, visit elderly neighbors, or when you have a pleasant conversation with the person behind you in the grocery store checkout line. How about doing something as simple as smiling at a stranger? You never know when something as simple as that might be the thing that makes that person's day and reinforces his belief that this old planet is an okay place to be.

Whatever your net worth is currently, it's only an assessment of your finances today. Not tomorrow, not forever. It's a place to build from. Remember, some people with assets and great wealth are very unhappy and unfulfilled. At the same time, others have six-figure assets, along with six-figure liabilities, and thus less net worth than the person with a $40,000 annual income.

Many of us have been heavily in debt for so long that we forget about some of our assets and minimize others because they are so overshadowed by our bills. Also, some of our assets are not liquid (meaning that we don't have access to them in the form of cash), so we think they don't count. Keep in mind that you've earned them and you need to recognize them and appreciate what you're building. Knowing your net worth generally gives you an emotional boost when you see the numbers and realize the value of the things you own. So let's face our fears and acknowledge our blessings by completing a balance sheet. It may feel a bit uncomfortable at first, but sit with those feelings and forge ahead. Don't allow yourself to feel shame or guilt about where you are today. If you've done the previous exercises in this book, you can rest assured that you're back on the track and building steam. We'll pick up speed when the time is right. But for now, be honest with yourself and don't leave anything out—assets or liabilities. Just list the amount of current market value for each asset. For example, your car's value would depreciate with use, but hopefully your real estate's value would go up. On the liabilities side, list the amounts currently owed for each item, such as the balance owing on your automobile or home improvement loan, not the cost of anticipated repairs or insurance payments. For our purposes, we're going to follow the acronym KISS (Keep It Simple, Sister).

Exercise One: Your Net Worth

Complete this statement and then fill in the amounts:

I, _____, as of this date, _____, acknowledge
that this is the state of my finances. It may not be where I'd like it to
be, but I know that it will improve from here. I am committed to getting my money straight, and completing this worksheet is another
step in my journey to financial health and peace of mind.

Signed _____

Assets:

Cash	_____
Checking accounts	_____
Savings accounts	_____
Certificates of deposits	_____
Stocks and bonds	_____
Money market funds	_____
Automobiles	_____
Mutual funds	_____
Primary real estate	_____
Income property	_____
IRA	_____
401K or 403B	_____
Total Assets	_____

Liabilities:

Credit cards	_____
Charge cards	_____
Automobiles	_____
Home improvement	_____
Credit union loans	_____
Student loans	_____
First mortgage	_____
Home equity loans	_____
Loans from family	_____
Loans from friends	_____
401K loan	_____
Past-due taxes	_____
Total Liabilities	_____

Any Add-Ons

Now that we have the basic items accounted for, use the following list to fine-
tune and add any other amounts to the appropriate side of the ledger:

- Cash value in life insurance
- Credit union checking or savings accounts
- Money owed to you by others
- Stock options
- Business interest
- Annuities (an investment from which one receives an income for
  a lifetime or a specified number of years)
- Tax-efficient savings plans
- Pensions
- Keogh or SEP (retirement plans for the self-employed)

- Household furnishings/antiques
- Art or collectibles
- Clothing and jewelry
- Life insurance loans
- Unimproved land

The Final Tally

Now, as a final step, do the last calculation to determine your net worth.

Total Assets	_____
Minus Total Liabilities	- _____
Equals Your Net Worth	_____

So, how does it feel? Is the amount more or less than you expected? What would you like it to be in three years, five years, and ten years? Record your reactions and emotions and write down any long-term goals that come to mind. Now I want you to make another commitment to yourself:

Exercise Two: Your Real Worth

Complete this statement and read it aloud each month after you balance your checkbook:

I, _____, promise to be proud of myself and to love myself for my financial accomplishments up to this point in my life. I know that whatever the state of my finances today, it is only a temporary situation. I am willing to be more attentive to my checkbook, realizing that my net worth will increase. I'll stay focused, consistent, and will have patience with myself and with the process. Most important, I'll feel good about myself because I know "I'm priceless."

Signed _____

Chapter Six

Prescription 3: Develop a Spending Plan

In 1976, a few months after I moved from Detroit to California, my younger brother, Walter, and sister, Paula, came out to visit me. Along with two cousins, Tracey and James, we decided to drive from Oakland to Los Angeles to pick up another friend, Marvin, who would hang out with us during their trip. I must say it seemed like a good idea at the time.

I was twenty-four and the others were teenagers between fourteen and nineteen. Today, I consider myself a reasonably intelligent person who understands the necessity of planning, but back then, I was young and naive. I didn't worry about many things because, after all, I was an independent woman—free, black, over twenty-one, and excited about living in California. I knew Los Angeles was a one-hour airplane ride and a simple drive south from the Bay Area. To get there we could take either State Highway 1 or Interstate Highway 5. Since I knew how to get to Highway 1 from San Francisco, the five of us piled into a rental car and hit the road on a beautiful Saturday morning about eight A.M. on our first ever automobile adventure.

Thirteen hours later, we arrived in Los Angeles, having had absolutely no clue it would take so long to complete the trip. Granted, it was an awesome experience given that Highway 1 meanders along the breathtakingly beautiful California coastline. But the route I had chosen consisted of narrow, mountainous winding roads with steep drop-offs into the deep blue Pacific Ocean. Thankfully, Walter took the wheel and the comedians in the car told jokes and funny stories that provided laughter and entertainment to sustain us throughout the journey. Yet during the last eight hours of the trip, a couple of my co-adventurers—namely my sister and brother—affectionately began to curse me because I'd had no idea of what I was getting them into. That was my first and last trip to Los Angeles on Highway 1.

The point is, had I even looked at a road map, asked a few questions, and gathered any information at all, I would have known there was an easier way to accomplish our goal. I would have especially known that Highway 5 was a five-hour road trip to Los Angeles on flat interstate.

Driving by the Seat of Our Pants

When it comes to finances, many of us take the same approach I did on my trip to L.A. We know where we want to go but drive or fly by the seat of our pants trying to get there. We haven't done our homework and have no concrete strategy on how to reach our destination—we just forge ahead blindly. When it comes to travel, a road map is a necessity, and when it comes to finances, a *spending plan* is the road map we need to get to our destination.

The spending plan, more commonly known as a budget, is in many ways *the* key prescription in getting our money straight. Often black women are put off by budgets because we don't want any ceilings put on our spending. A budget is like someone telling us how to spend our money, and we don't have time for that. The term *budget* has a negative connotation and feels limiting, restricting, and more or less cast in stone with no flexibility because we commit to it on paper. We work too hard to feel lack, deprivation, or extreme sacrifice. We also fear making a budget because it might show that we don't have enough money to meet all our wants and needs. Or because we're afraid to face our out-of-control spending patterns. Since most of us have on some occasion tried to follow a budget, it also feels like a setup for failure.

A spending plan, on the other hand, feels more positive. By definition, a plan is always proactive and empowering. You have choices in how you spend your money. Instead of tightening up and restricting ourselves, we approach this plan of estimated expenses and income with a sense of openness. The purpose of the spending plan is not to limit our spending but to identify what we need for a quality of life that has a sense of balance and well-being. It's a blueprint to help keep our financial house in order.

How to Develop a Spending Plan

A new spending plan should be developed for each month, detailed with your actual month's expenditures, and be completed at least fifteen days before the month starts. A very helpful if slightly more ambitious exercise is to create three additional spending plans for reference: a basic minimum, an average month, and an ideal month. The basic minimum plan details the worst-case scenario by identifying the least amount of money you can get by on during any given month. The average-month plan is where you factor in an amortized amount in every category of spending. For example, you may not buy new clothes each month, but let's say that over the course of the year, you generally spend $1,200 on clothing. In the average-month plan, you would calculate $100 each month to be set aside to cover the cost of new clothing when the purchases are actually made. Under the ideal plan, you complete the worksheet using the ideal amount you would like to spend in each category.

Now, don't go too crazy when you complete the ideal plan. We could all come up with a $20,000 spending plan for the month if we let our imaginations fly. At some point, you should be daring and make a "no holds barred" plan just to see what it would cost to meet all your needs and wants if money were no object. But for our purposes right now, I'm suggesting you use some degree of reason when you complete the ideal plan. Think about what it would take for you to eat out as often as you'd like, or tithe a full 10 percent to your church, or allocate a monthly amount to give to your parents each month, just to help them out. How much money would you need to earn in order to make this ideal plan a reality? It's something to think about and can also be very helpful if you're planning a job change. It might give you a starting point for negotiating a new salary.

Take a Look at the Bennies

The spending plan has many benefits. When you add up all your expenses and subtract that figure from your net income, it leaves your cash flow. If the figure is zero, you basically break even for the month—and that's good. At least you know all of your needs for the month can be met without using any credit cards to supplement your income. Often when we have not created a spending plan, our imagination starts to run wild as the bills pile up and we feel anxious and uncomfortable, thinking, "There's not going to be enough." But having a grasp of the actual numbers lets you know, "If I do what I've outlined here, I can take care of myself and there should be no financial problems for the month." This clarity is invaluable. You begin to replace anxiety with hopefulness and self-confidence. You now know you have the ability to take care of yourself and meet your basic needs.

Even some of the most highly educated black women are intimidated, resistant, or fearful at the thought of being proactive in anticipating their future expenditures. Granted, some women would rather avoid dealing with a money plan as long as possible. But when the inevitable emergency occurs, we are forced to react. Unfortunately, the decisions we make under duress tend to lack clarity and sound judgment. For example, let's say the transmission goes out on your eight-year-old Nissan Maxima, and the repair will cost $1,500. In a panic you put the charge on your American Express card. You know the bill will have to be paid in full, but you feel you have no other choice because you need your car for work. That's when the stress begins. When properly skilled at using the spending plan, you can avoid anxiety and make fiscally sound choices without creating repercussions to be dealt with later. You should accept the fact that as long as you live, unexpected things are going to happen. But you don't have to throw your finances into chaos and become overwhelmed each time—and the spending plan can help avoid that.

Rachel's Spending Plan

Remember Rachel, the sister with the checkbook and debt problems who did such a fabulous job of getting her money straight in Chapter Five? Let's take a look at her actual spending plan to see what her cash flow was like when she started her financial healing. Here's what we came up with:

Monthly Spending Plan			
Food		**Recovery/Self-Improvement**	
Groceries	145	Spiritual	20
Breakfast	10	**Total**	**20**
Lunch	25		
Total	**180**	**Dependent Care**	
		Children's Charities	24
Shelter		**Total**	**24**
Mortgage	875		
Homeowner's Dues	170	**Transportation**	
Phone	30	Gas	33
Gas and Electric	30	Parking/Tolls	1
Cable	26	Bus	60
Newspaper	20	Car wash	4
Household Items	20	**Total**	**98**
Insurance	20		
Total	**1,191**		

Self-Care		Entertainment	
Clothing	50	Movies	8
Hair care	100	Books	30
Medical	30	Dance Class	50
Dry Cleaners/Laundry	20	**Total**	**88**
Gym	50		
Total	**250**	Miscellaneous	
		Birthday Gift	20
Debt Repayment		Internet	15
Sears	20	**Total**	**35**
Visa	120		
Macy's	80		
Totals	**220**		

Cash on Hand	-340*
Total Income	2,450
Total Expenses	2,106
Cash Flow	4

* This is the amount of money we start off with in addition to our monthly income. In Rachel's case, it's negative due to the fact that she owed money for the previous payroll deposit error.

Rachel's spending plan ended up with positive cash flow. That means if she sticks to the plan, she'll have $4 left over at the end of the month. Her cash flow would have been greater if she hadn't had to replace the funds she used in the payroll deposit error. Otherwise she could have had $344 available at the end of the month. But based on her historical spending patterns, she likely would have frittered that away on clothing or other impulse purchases.

If this were your spending plan and you had $344 left over at the end of the month, what would you do with it? Save it? Spend it? Pay debt with it? There's no wrong answer. But let me make a few suggestions, because it doesn't have to be an all-or-nothing decision.

First, consider any categories or areas of spending for which you've conservatively allocated funds for the month. For instance, your money has been tight for so long that you didn't realize you literally have only one pair of wool slacks to wear to work and it's already November. While keeping your goals in mind, you might want to add $75 to $100 to the clothing estimate. Review each line item in the spending plan and determine if you need to increase any other area.

Next, consider your savings cushion. How much cash do you have set aside in savings that you have easy access to? It doesn't matter if it's $500 or $5,000. The amount will vary from person to person. What's important is that the amount feel somewhat comfortable to cover any emergencies you might have.

Finally, look at debt repayment as an area to make good use of the positive cash flow. Any additional contributions to this area will only help you to liquidate your obligations faster and reach your goal to be debt free sooner.

Exercise One: Your Own Spending Plan

Now it's time for you to create your Spending Plan. This is a major exercise that occupies most of the rest of this chapter. If you're reading this in the spring or summertime, pause a few minutes to fix yourself a glass of iced tea or lemonade. If it's fall or wintertime, take a break to brew a cup of hot tea, coffee, or chocolate. Now, with your glass or cup within arm's reach, sit back and relax, because we're going to take our time and do this exercise step by step.

Step 1: Getting Ready

To complete your Spending Plan, you'll be estimating your personal and business expenses for the upcoming month. The following worksheet from *The Basic Money Management Workbook* provides an easy, detailed format to work with. To start, take out your calendar or Palm Pilot so that you can see what activities you have scheduled for the upcoming month that will require cash. Don't forget to use a pencil so you can erase rather than scratch out. Also, place your Goal Worksheet from Chapter Four in front of you along with photos or pictures of your goals. Use these tools to help you keep your perspective on your monthly spending. With each discretionary dollar you allocate, you should weigh the importance of that expenditure against your stated goals.

Get ready to go through the detailed monthly Spending Plan, estimating the amount of money you expect to spend in each area. Pay special attention to any category you really struggle with, because it may be a sign of unresolved internal conflict. For example, Rhonda, a thirty-four-year-old security guard, could not get past the first category—groceries. While being coached through the plan, she became very teary. We discovered that as a child, Rhonda wasn't nourished properly and there were lots of fights in her family at the dinner table. As an adult, she still hesitated to buy sufficient food for herself, never had much food in her refrigerator, and felt guilty whenever she went out to eat. After several sessions of talking about this difficulty, Rhonda realized her early experiences had left her feeling unworthy of eating the foods she needed for good nutrition and undeserving of the foods she enjoyed for their taste and texture. I suggested she gradually overcome those feelings by adding in just one new grocery item per month. That way she did not feel overwhelming guilt, but instead was able to see gradually and safely that it was okay to allocate enough money to groceries and give herself permission to be well fed.

Here are some of the categories you'll encounter:

Food. In this category, most of us are unaware of how much money we actually spend. The reality usually exceeds what we think. We may feel we spend $200 for food because that's the amount we allocate for groceries. But we forget about the midweek trips to the store as well as cash spent for daily lunches and afternoon snacks at the vending machine. Be sure to include any amounts spent on weekends, for take-out foods, and for pizza delivery.

Housing. List your mortgage, rent, or whatever you estimate as your monthly expense for housing. Don't include expenses that are not due for this particular month. For example, if a utility bill comes quarterly, list it only during the month you plan to pay it. Don't forget about expenses for the gardener, burglar alarm system, or storage fees.

Household Items. Calculate money spent on garbage bags, paper towels, cleaning supplies, lightbulbs, and other nonfood items you buy for the house. If you operate a computer at home, include printer ink cartridges, fax machine paper, and any other supplies you may need to replenish during the current month.

Self-Care. Include amounts for the gym, chiropractor, eyeglasses, hair care, and other miscellaneous expenses having to do with your physical and personal upkeep. If your life, health, and disability premiums are deducted from your paycheck, do not include them here. Right now we're working only with your net income (the amount after taxes and other deductions).

Recovery/Self-Improvement. Write down what you tithe at church and/or what you spend on a therapist, seminars, continuing education, or support groups. Remember to include books, magazines, tapes, workshops, seminars, and any other self-help activities or expenses.

Dependent Care. Be sure to list everything you are spending for your children, parents, or anyone else who is dependent upon you. Make allocations for tuition, allowances, classes, tutors, and any spending money you provide to the kids.

Transportation. Write in an amount for gas, taxi expenses, car washes, maintenance, and repairs. Don't forget fares for the bus, streetcar, rapid transit train, or subway.

Entertainment. Make sure you maintain balance in your life by planning to have some fun even if funds are tight. Add a line for CDs, records, books, and video rental, including late fees. Also, vacation expenses should be added to this category if money will be spent during the current month.

Savings and Investments. Three months of living expenses are recommended as a savings cushion. But that amount could equal several thousand dollars and feel too overwhelming right now to attain. What's important is to develop a consistent savings program even if it's only a small amount, such as $10 or $20 monthly. As your cash flow improves, you can increase the amount. Use this area for money being set aside for future vacations. Complete the retirement line only if you contribute funds from your net income. Also, any contributions to an investment club should be noted in this area.

Monthly Allocation. Use this section for property taxes, income taxes, or any large sum of money that you need to set aside in advance.

Miscellaneous. This is the place for any items that don't seem to fit into other categories, such as charitable giving (other than church), postage, and gifts you plan to give during the current month.

Debt Repayment. To start out, let's use minimum payments in this area to make sure that we keep each account current. Later, when you have determined the amount of positive cash flow this month, go back and increase the payments to an appropriate amount.

One-Time Expenses. Use this area if you anticipate an expense that is typically nonrecurring—for example, a major fence repair or replacement of a basic piece of household furniture.

Business Expenses. Write in all expenses even if they are to be reimbursed later. If your money needs to be spent in advance, we need to account for it.

Income. Fill in the amount of your net salary. Also, include any business reimbursements expected or other funds that might be used to pay your expenses. Be sure to add any money you plan to transfer from savings.

Step 2: Fill in the Blanks

As you complete your spending plan, make the best estimate you can of your upcoming needs. Be honest with yourself as you reflect on your spending patterns. You may end up spending more or less in a given category, but for now make your best guess. We'll adjust the numbers later if we have to. And don't worry about what the amounts are adding up to. After you've completed the worksheet, go back and calculate the totals for each category.

First, let's go through and only fill in the estimated amounts in column 2 for each line item in column 1 on the spending plan. How much do you need to spend in each area to make you feel whole and complete? For example, let's say you generally spend $50 each Friday in the grocery store. Next month there are four Fridays, so you'll estimate $200 for the month. Then go to the next line (breakfast) and continue down the entire list.

Okay, are you ready to get started? If you're feeling anxious or fearful, let's take one additional step. To establish a calm, healthy mind-set before you begin to create your spending plan, do a quiet meditation. Get comfortable in your chair, relax, breathe deeply, and accept the idea that this process is designed to meet your need to feel whole and complete. Let go of all feelings of limitation. Repeat the following meditation:

"There is nothing in all the world for me to fear. For greater is the miracle working power of the Holy Spirit than any other appearance. All of my wants and needs are met because God (or whomever you believe in) is my source." All is well and so it is.

Now just take it one step at a time and remember to keep breathing!

Monthly Spending Plan

	mo. plan	wk. 1	wk. 2	wk. 3	wk. 4	wk. 5	mo. total
Food							
Groceries							
Breakfast							
Lunch							
Dinner							
Snacks							
Guest							
Totals							
Shelter							
Housing							
Phone							
Water/Garbage							
Gas and Electric							
Cable							
Newspaper							
Household Items							
Insurance							
Housekeeper							
Totals							
Self-Care							
Clothing							
Shoes							
Accessories							
Hair Care							
Toiletries							
Manicure							
Massage							
Medical							
Dry Cleaners/Laundry							
Life/Disability Insurance							
Totals							
Recovery/Self-Improvement							
Spiritual							
Therapy							
Financial Counseling							
Totals							

	mo. plan	wk. 1	wk. 2	wk. 3	wk. 4	wk. 5	mo. total
Dependent Care							
Clothes							
Child Care							
Pets							
Totals							
Transportation							
Car Payment							
Gas							
Maintenance							
Parking/Tolls							
Bus or Other							
Insurance							
Totals							
Entertainment							
Movies							
Video Rental							
Concerts/Theater							
Dating							
Totals							
Investments							
Savings (Cushion)							
Vacation							
Retirement							
Totals							
Monthly Allocations							
Taxes							
Car Registration							
Totals							
Miscellaneous							
Totals							

	mo. plan	wk. 1	wk. 2	wk. 3	wk. 4	wk. 5	mo. total
Debt Repayment							
Totals							
One-Time Expenses							
Totals							
Business Expenses							
Rent							
Phone							
Office Supplies							
Postage							
Totals							
Income							
Totals							

How are you doing so far? Are you still breathing normally, or are you feeling a bit anxious? Take a moment to stretch, relax your muscles, and breathe deeply before you proceed. If you've come this far, you're doing great. I'm proud of you, and you should be proud of yourself too. Let's move on.

Now that you have completed each line item with a sufficient amount to meet your needs, add these estimated expenses by category if you haven't already done so. If you have more than one source of income expected for the month, be sure to total the income column as well. Next, take the monthly plan totals for each category and fill in the monthly Category Recap below to determine your total expenses and planned cash flow for the month. Pay particular attention to the cash-on-hand figure—that is, the amount of money you are going to start the month with before you receive any paychecks. For now, calculate your cash on hand by estimating how much money you expect to have left over at the end of the month. Include money in your wallet, petty cash at home, and checking account balances. In the unlikely event that your checkbook will have a negative balance (I know this is highly unlikely because of your commitment to the Helpful Hints in Chapter Five), you must indicate the negative amount as cash on hand because you are starting the month in the hole—just as Rachel did on her spending plan.

Category Recap

Food	_____
Shelter	_____
Self-Care	_____
Recovery/Self-Improvement	_____
Dependent Care	_____
Transportation	_____
Entertainment	_____
Investments	_____
Monthly Allocations	_____
Miscellaneous	_____
Debt Repayment	_____
One-Time Expenses	_____
Business Expenses	_____
Total Expenses	_____

Cash on Hand		_____
Income	+	_____
Total Monthly Income	=	_____
Total Expenses	-	_____
Cash Flow	=	_____

Give It a Gander

Well, how does it look to you? Now, don't panic if your expenses exceed your income. Eight out of ten of my clients have a negative cash flow the first time we prepare a spending plan. Since we create the plan not looking solely at what you expect to pay, but instead at how much money you need to spend in order to feel whole and complete, it's not unusual that those two amounts differ. What this negative cash flow indicates is that there needs to be an increase in income. Of course, I know that's not news for most people. What is news, though, is finding out exactly *how much* additional money it will take to meet our monthly needs. With this specific knowledge, you can now focus with clarity on the goal. If the cash flow is negative $200, we know that by increasing our income by $200, all of our monthly needs will be met.

Another thing that is usually quite noticeable when a client completes a spending plan is how much money is spent daily on breakfast, lunch, dinner, and snacks. When we get honest with ourselves, we are usually shocked to see how a few dollars here and a few dollars there add up quickly. One client totaled up the amount of money she spent at vending machines on soft drinks and chips for her afternoon break each day. When she realized the total amount, she shrieked, "My God, I could use that forty dollars to make my Visa payment!"

Another couple didn't realize until they completed a spending plan that they forked over $100 per month on cappuccino. That comes to $1,200 each year! And that's conservative. Most people who drink coffee have at least one cup daily. At $3 a pop, multiplied by 365 days a year, one person could easily spend $1,095. This is not to pass judgment on how you spend your money. But it's important that you know where your money's going. This way you can decide if cappuccino is a higher priority in your life than your stated goal to keep your kids in private school or to buy a second car.

If your spending plan indicated a negative cash flow, don't immediately think "How can I cut back?" Noted psychologist and business consultant Dr. Fred Grosse, who is known for helping people double their income in one year, says, "Increase your income to meet your dreams rather than shrink your dreams to fit the budget." So let's begin by exploring the options for increasing your income first.

Exercise Two: Think of Ways to Bring in More Money

Take a piece of paper and spend fifteen minutes brainstorming ways to add to your income. Before you begin, take a deep breath and repeat the affirmation "Abundance is my birthright" several times out loud. Here are a few ideas to get you started. What about . . .

Overtime? If you work at a job where overtime is available, putting in a few extra hours can make the difference between meeting your needs and being in deprivation. It doesn't mean you have to make this a permanent part of your life, but it's a viable option, especially when you know exactly how much money it will take to eliminate your negative cash flow. Calculate how many hours you'd need to work to cover your shortfall and determine if working overtime is possible.

Pay increase? When your expenses exceed your income on a consistent basis, it may be time to ask for a pay raise. Assess your job performance and your job skills and be prepared to ask for what you're worth.

Job promotion? Realizing the need to cover negative cash flow might be just the thing to spur your ambition to another level. Having a desire to alter your lifestyle may necessitate taking on more responsibility in order to generate more income. Be open to the possibilities.

Changing jobs? If you've hit the income ceiling or are not satisfied with your current employer, it's possible you're not as productive as you could be in your work environment. It may be time to consider a job change to reinvigorate your professional life and increase your cash flow.

Collecting outstanding debts? Sometimes when people owe us money, we simply write off the debt because we're too embarrassed to ask for it to be repaid. As black women, our caring, supportive nature can cause us to enable others who owe us money. Be sure to ask those who owe for repayment of any loans that are outstanding or a commitment to a repayment program.

Part-time employment? I believe spending eight, ten, or twelve hours per day on a job is ample time to be away from our families and loved ones. Besides that, I think we need to allow sufficient time for rest and recuperation. So I'm not a big proponent of getting part-time jobs. But if your cash flow is negative, consider working part-time on a temporary basis as you set goals and develop strategies to increase your regular income.

Exercise Three: Think of Ways to Stretch Your Income

If bringing in more money seems unrealistic, you can often combat negative cash flow just by stretching your current income. You'll be amazed at how a little ingenuity can extend your dollars and prevent you from having to cut back on the things that keep you happy and fulfilled. Now, take fifteen minutes and brainstorm ways to stretch your money. This is an excellent exercise even if you don't have negative cash flow—stretching those dollars in creative ways can free up cash to put toward paying off debt or those dream goals, such as a new home or a vacation. You might try:

Bartering or trading for services. All of us have talents and gifts to offer to the world. Identify what yours are and consider using them to trade for services. One of my clients was good at janitorial work and offered to clean the floors at her local beauty salon in exchange for haircuts for her entire family.

Reducing the frequency of purchases. Just because your cash flow for the month is negative doesn't mean you have to completely eliminate certain areas of spending. Be open to modification. For example, if your pattern is to get a manicure weekly, change it to two times per month and learn to maintain your nails in between.

Getting a roommate. We all love our privacy and don't particularly relish the idea of sharing our space with someone other than a mate. However, a roommate is a very viable option to consider on a temporary basis. When I started my business, I realized that leasing a house and separate office space was too much to carry while also trying to pay off $50,000 in debt. I decided to go into a house-share arrangement. In essence, I rented half a house from the homeowner. I had two bedrooms and a bathroom for my private space and we shared the living room, dining room, and kitchen. Originally, I thought this arrangement would work for me for a year or two. In reality, it lasted eight years. We shared two different houses, and it worked out great for both of us—long enough for me to pay off my debt, get my business on solid ground, and save enough money to purchase my next home. Be open to temporary situations that can help you achieve your permanent goals.

Changing transportation. Ideally, we'd like to make things as convenient for ourselves as possible. Driving to work falls into that category. But when looking for ways to reduce expenses, explore taking the bus or the rapid transit system instead of driving and spending money for gasoline and parking. Also, look for opportunities to carpool or ride-share to cut down on expenses.

Reviewing deductions. Reassess the money being withheld from your paycheck. You don't want to owe income taxes come April 15, but you also don't need to look forward to a large refund check when you're struggling to make ends meet on a monthly basis. Although I strongly recommend fully participating in 401K plans, you might consider reducing your contributions temporarily until you get your cash flow positive again.

Using consignment. Most sisters have closets so stuffed with clothes and shoes that we hardly have room for new things. Clear the clutter from your closets and take any salable items to consignment shops. One professional sister put on consignment five shopping bags of clothing and suits she no longer wore and returned to the shop a month later to have over $500 waiting for her!

Having a yard sale. You'd be amazed at how other people value things you deem totally insignificant. When moving from one home to another, I always try to ensure that I'm not taking anything that I don't intend to use within the next six months—no matter how large or how small. At one yard sale I had a box of promotional items from my former bank such as paperweights, clocks, and knickknacks. One customer at the yard sale was delighted and purchased them all. Initially, I wondered, Why would she want these old things? Turns out she was a retired employee from the bank and didn't have those particular mementos in her collection.

Income Tips for Entrepreneurs

If you happen to be an entrepreneur and have a fluctuating income, there are some additional things you will want to do. The spending plan lets you know what it takes to meet your needs for the month, just like a wage-earning employee. I suggest you complete a basic minimum plan so you can focus on not letting your income be less than that amount. If you don't have at least this amount as your goal, you'll move aimlessly through the month and tend to either struggle regularly or have large income swings.

Suzanne, from Chapter Three, is one of my most successful entrepreneurial clients. She embraced early on an idea that I shared with her. I had always encouraged her to strive for consistency so that she didn't have enormous peaks and valleys in her income and corresponding peaks and valleys in her emotions. But more important, as we'd complete her spending plans, I would simply say, "You know, you can always make more money." That's the beauty of being an entrepreneur—your income is in your hands. That let her know that her actual and ideal needs could be met because of her income potential. She ultimately met and far exceeded all expectations. Over a seven-year period she went from $30,000 to $160,000 per year in annual income by planning, setting goals, and aggressively marketing her business!

Once your income no longer fluctuates lower than your basic minimum spending plan, and you have months where you are flush with cash, that's the time to set money aside to build your reserves. It's crucial to save money during this period in order to supplement any future lapses in income.

Exercise Four: Look at Possible Reductions

Only after you have taken all the things listed above into consideration is it time to take another step to alleviate the remaining negative cash flow. Start with groceries again and review the plan line by line. If possible, reduce the estimates by an additional amount—large or small—and hopefully without going into deprivation. Strive to take $5 off here, $10 off there, and $20 in the next place. It may seem like these small amounts are too nominal to make a difference, but you'd be surprised at how they add up. Also, determine if any expense can be put off until next month. One client, Jane, played a little game with herself. She explained: "I put some time and space between the desire to make a purchase and completing the monthly Spending Plan, and tell myself I'll get the item next month. Then, when next month comes, I don't feel the same urgency and can usually get by without spending the money."

Another strategy is to think in terms of reducing the frequency of some purchases. For example, if your pattern is to buy lunch five times a week, change it to three times per week and pack a lunch the other days. At age thirty-seven, Ethel had earned a good income for several years and was used to spending her money indiscriminately. Packing a lunch was not something she was willing to consider until she set a goal to buy her first home. Soon after implementing this strategy, she found taking her lunch helped her stick to her nutritional food plan as well as save money.

Once you've totally eliminated the negative cash flow, review the plan one final time to make sure it's balanced and that there is no deprivation in any one area. If there is, it will likely cause you to binge in another. Also, if your partner or mate was not involved in the process up to this point, be sure to share the plan with him. Ask for his cooperation, but realize you have no control over what he does. Your objective is to adhere to the plan that you've created and focus on staying the course "one day at a time."

Prioritizing Your Payments

If you have taken all the steps listed above and still have a negative cash flow, don't dismay. It's known to happen, especially when a substantial amount of one's income goes toward debt repayment. Generally, I recommend paying your bills using the following priorities:

Food. Obviously, you and your family have to eat to stay alive and healthy. That doesn't mean you need to overeat or to consume only gourmet foods.

Shelter. If you're alive you need a place to live (a luxury home, weekly housekeeper, and monthly cable television service are not, however, basic necessities). If your finances have been tight for a while, you may find yourself in a position where some of your basic expenses such as rent or utility bills are past due. If this is the case, when completing your spending plan, you should initially include the full amount to bring the account current and see how it affects your bottom line. For example, let's say you are two months behind on your electricity bill. If paying the balance in full results in a negative cash flow, recalculate the plan using one and a half payments. Then contact the company to verify that they will accept this amount for two months. At that point you'll be current.

Transportation. You'll need some form of wheels to get back and forth to work in order to continue to generate income. They don't, however, have to be Lexus or BMW wheels. They can be more modest Ford Escort or Volkswagen Jetta wheels. Or they can even be publicly owned wheels, especially if you live in a major city where good bus, streetcar, or rapid transit systems are readily available.

Dependent Care. If other family members, particularly children, are financially dependent on you, there is no way to avoid these expenses. And this is not the area in which to cut corners. With child care in particular, you get what you pay for, so good, safe, loving day-care providers are a necessity for your kids' well-being as well as your own peace of mind. However, you can find decent child care without paying Cadillac prices. Also, if a relative is available to watch your offspring at little or no cost, that's wonderful. But treat the relative the same way you would a professional. Don't take advantage by being late every day or adding on extra days, or the relatives may eventually declare themselves no longer available.

Self-Care, Recovery, Entertainment, and Investments. I generally lump this group together as the fourth area of priority because they are critical to taking care of yourself.

And, Finally, Debt Repayment. Here there is some flexibility regarding payments that will be fully explained in Chapter Eight: "Pay Off Debt with Discipline—Not Deprivation."

Congratulations on a Job Well Done

Generally, there is a real sense of relief after creating a Spending Plan. How you'll meet your needs will have become visible. Fear subsides for a while. If two hours or two weeks later tension rears its ugly head again, you can look at the numbers and know that everything is still okay. You may feel anxious about it, but follow the plan anyway and make a commitment to do a new plan each month. We'll discuss tracking and analyzing the results in the next chapter. What is important right now is that you stick with the plan, because "it will work if you work it." You might even make a copy of the plan and place it on your refrigerator door just as a reminder to stay the course. Above all, be gentle with yourself. These are new prescriptive behaviors designed to break old habits and cure financial ills. For best results, give the medication time to work.

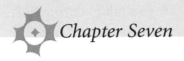

Chapter Seven

Prescription 4: Track and Analyze Your Spending

Through the open window I could hear Mattie whistling as she pranced up the walkway to my office for our monthly financial counseling appointment. As I opened the door, I was greeted by a huge smile and a big hug from my client, who was sporting yet another new look. Today, thirty-six-year-old Mattie had shoulder-length braids curled in tight little ringlets that bounced up and down as she made her way through the waiting room and took a seat in my office.

Mattie started in full of energy and enthusiasm: "I'm excited about tracking my spending."

"Well, I'm excited for you," I responded. Then she proudly handed me a dozen or so worksheets that represented the tracking she had done for the past twelve months. "Congratulations on such a great accomplishment," I said. "And what do you feel you've learned from all of this work?" Without hesitation, Mattie replied, "The first thing I did was look at my totals and say out loud, 'I spent *how much* on my hair? Oh, no. This won't do. I don't like spending that much time or money on hair!'"

As African Americans, we place an awful lot of emphasis on our hair and take great delight today in having so much versatility with it. In a two-year period, I had seen Mattie go from a short natural, to cornrows, coils, braids—everything except a human hair weave. I don't mean to sound judgmental. There's nothing wrong with it, because she had fun doing it. But there was a trade-off. Because of the hairstyling and other things that were made a priority, Mattie reluctantly had to share a two-bedroom apartment with a much older woman who had house rules that prohibited Mattie from fully enjoying her living space. Soon after she first came to see me, we set a goal, and after creating spending plans and tracking her cash flow for one year, Mattie saw how she could afford to live alone. Then she took a big step and got her own apartment.

Like many other single black women, Mattie thought for years that she couldn't afford a place of her own. And forget about trying to buy a home. Even with a steady job she had difficulty believing she could ever handle a mortgage payment on her own and felt intimidated at the thought of dealing with lenders who would see the blemishes on her credit report. But now, after consistently tracking her spending for another year, Mattie is feeling confident because she knows where her money is going. She's ready to take another step up the ladder of success and purchase her first home. After religiously tracking every cent she earned last year, she can visibly see areas of spending that she's willing to modify in order to acquire her dream, including hair, travel, and self-improvement, to name a few.

Where Does Your Money Go?

"Glinda, I make good money, but I just don't know where it goes!" That's the number-one comment I hear from new clients seeking financial counseling. This is true whether they make a lot of money or a little. By not knowing where the money goes we lose our power over it and tend to feel insecure. The vagueness leads us to mentally chastise ourselves by saying, "Why don't I have more to show for all the years I've been working? Why don't I have more money in retirement savings? What's wrong with me?"

Knowing what's happening with our money can often be stressful as well. We may feel guilty, apprehensive, or resistant to looking at how the choices we've made have affected our finances, and at the deep-seated emotions that drove those choices. Such was the case for Malia when she was faced with an unexpected divorce.

With her hair done in neat cornrows, dressed in a conservative and well-tailored suit, forty-year-old Malia had an authoritative air about her despite her soft voice. The mother of two had worked as a bank manager for fifteen years, during which time she and her husband, a municipal judge, had acquired a comfortable home and rental property.

But Malia's security had been shaken three years earlier, when her husband walked out on her and the two kids, filed for divorce, and then quickly remarried. "After the divorce, I was in such shock that I didn't watch my money, and the debts piled up," she said. Malia's emotional trauma had caused her to become disconnected from her finances, and for a while she refused to concentrate on them. Unfortunately, before she knew it, the spending resulted in several thousand dollars in new debt. "I can't really say what I've been spending on these past few years," Malia admitted when she first came to my office. "I haven't been frivolous, but I need to do something about it before it gets too far out of hand."

Malia, like many black women in this country, had to deal with taking care of her children and getting on with her life after the divorce. In her efforts to minimize the trauma and maintain a sense of stability for her kids, she chose to keep the house in the divorce settlement. That decision alone largely created the basis for her shaky finances. She was now trying to maintain virtually the same household on a single salary. Had she tracked and analyzed her expenses over a period of time, she would have known what it would take to meet her financial needs. By exploring different scenarios such as staying in the house, buying a smaller house, or moving to an apartment, she would have realized that staying in the house left no wiggle room in her budget for emergencies or unplanned expenses. In fact, even with child support, the basics were barely covered. Every extracurricular school activity, weekend getaway, and car repair necessitated a major financial juggling act.

Being able to account for your finances is important. But it's impossible to be accountable if you don't actually track your spending or have a system for knowing what's happening to your money. There is a simple way to resolve this problem—write down every cent you spend. I know you've heard it before. You may have even done it for a week or two at some point in the past. But generally, that's not long enough if you're serious about getting your money straight. Recording for a longer period, along with analyzing the results, is bound to reveal some things you didn't know or confirm some things you suspected about your money habits. It's not that you need to track every cent you spend for the rest of your life, but you do need to do it for several months, preferably for one year, to get an accurate indication of your patterns and the seasonal changes that take place with your expenditures and lifestyle needs.

"Tracking my spending remains a valuable and necessary part of my financial program," says Suzanne, the sister whose family tree was described in Chapter Two. She continues to track her spending seven years after her first financial counseling session (granted, with a few breaks in between). Now that she makes more money, of course, there's a tendency to spend more. "Last year I spent money like I was pouring it through a sieve. I remained conscious of my spending the entire time, but tracking and analyzing helped me know where I was going, and that's what makes the difference for me. If I don't know where I'm going, I can't take action and make decisions."

Tracking Made Easy

If you're like me, you probably live by your calendar, Franklin Planner, or Palm Pilot. In my case, there's so much going on that I can't be certain of what I'm supposed to do or what I've done unless I look at my calendar. Because it's almost always with me, the calendar is the best place I have found to initially track my spending. In years past, I couldn't remember how much money I had spent, or where, at the end of the day. The "easy" ATM money was the hardest to keep track of. If I withdrew $40 from the ATM, by evening I'd be trying to figure out why I had only $27.55 in my wallet. Invariably, I would forget about stopping to spend $4.50 for dry cleaning, $3.20 for postage, $3.63 for a snack, and $2.00 for a bridge toll. That comes to $12.45 for the day. Granted, I might not purchase exactly the same items every day, but over the course of the month, that kind of spending equals about $400 unaccounted for if it's not recorded and almost $5,000 a year.

There are a number of options available to track your daily expenses. I suggest you use the one that you like the best and are more motivated to use consistently. The following are some tools you can use to record expenses as they occur:

- Calendars, organizers, and Palm Pilots—Most of these have an expense section that you can use to list your daily expenditures. If not, write the amount of any spending in the memo area or on the page that represents the day money was spent. Expenses paid by cash, check, or credit card should all be noted.

- Receipts—Get into the habit of asking for receipts every time you spend money. If you choose this method, carry an envelope in your purse to put the receipts in. Otherwise, you'll have a cluttered, unorganized handbag that breeds a cluttered, unorganized financial life.

- Envelopes—If you use the receipt method above, you could also write the amount of any small cash purchases that have no receipt directly on the envelope.

- Spiral notebooks—A small spiral notebook can be purchased at most drugstores to keep track of your daily spending. Because of its size, it can easily fit into a wallet or be carried in a small clutch purse.

- Checkbook registers—This is one of my favorite tools to use in initially tracking my expenses. Checks used to make purchases are already listed there, and any item bought with cash is probably ATM money drawn from the same account, so I use the memo line to show where the money went.

The Tracking Worksheet

The following worksheet is designed to allow you to easily track and analyze your daily expenses. Rather than writing in this book, make some photocopies ahead of time—one for each week of the month. Or consider obtaining *The Basic Money Management Workbook,* which is a good companion to this book because it contains Spending Plans and tracking sheets for a twelve-month period. In any case, track your spending, and then transfer the amounts to the worksheet at the end of the day. I recommend keeping the worksheet visible on your nightstand to ensure you complete it. If tracking goes undone for a few days, there's a tendency to say, "Oh, forget it. I'll start again next month." But don't do that. Re-create what you can, then start tracking again. As explained previously, the manual system forces you to connect with your money. But you can also consider using Excel to design your own spreadsheet.

Since the purpose of tracking is to know where your money is going, we need to account for everything you buy. Sometimes you pay with cash, and we definitely need to track that. Other times you write checks or use a debit card, and that gets recorded in your check register. But let's say you buy $10 worth of gasoline using your credit card. At this point, the $10 is not coming out of your cash flow for the month, so should you write it down? Absolutely. But make a special

Daily Tracking

	mon	tue	wed	thu	fri	sat	sun	total
Food								
Groceries								
Breakfast								
Lunch								
Dinner								
Snacks								
Guest								
Totals								
Shelter								
Housing								
Phone								
Water/Garbage								
Gas and Electric								
Cable								
Newspaper								
Household Items								
Insurance								
Housekeeper								
Totals								
Self-Care								
Clothing								
Shoes								
Accessories								
Hair Care								
Toiletries								
Manicure								
Massage								
Medical								
Dry Cleaners/Laundry								
Life/Disability Insurance								
Totals								
Recovery/Self-Improvement								
Spiritual								
Therapy								
Financial Counseling								
Totals								

	mon	tue	wed	thu	fri	sat	sun	total
Dependent Care								
Clothes								
Child Care								
Pets								
Totals								
Transportation								
Car Payment								
Gas								
Maintenance								
Parking/Tolls								
Bus or Other								
Insurance								
Totals								
Entertainment								
Movies								
Video Rental								
Concerts/Theater								
Dating								
Totals								
Investments								
Savings (Cushion)								
Vacation								
Retirement								
Totals								
Monthly Allocations								
Taxes								
Car Registration								
Totals								
Miscellaneous								
Totals								

	mon	tue	wed	thu	fri	sat	sun	total
Debt Repayment								
Totals								
One-Time Expenses								
Totals								
Business Expenses								
Rent								
Phone								
Office Supplies								
Postage								
Totals								
Income								
Totals								

notation that it was charged. We want to account for it but not in the same way as with cash purchases. Put "cc" next to the amount, circle it, or possibly color-code it to indicate it was paid with a credit card. The actual payment of this item will show up under Debt Repayment, but tracking in this way will allow you to know how much money is paid out and where it's going.

Tracking may seem like a lot of work, but eventually it becomes second nature. If you stay on top of it, you're less likely to get overwhelmed and frustrated. "But I don't have time to do this!" some of you might be saying right now. True, time is a factor for all of us. But we also know that we make time for the things that are important to us. Tracking really doesn't take as much time as you think. Do you have three minutes a day? That's all it will take to jot down the four or five places where you spent money during the course of an average day. Do you have fifteen minutes a week? You won't need much more than that to total up your spending for the week by category. Finally, do you have thirty minutes at the end of the month? You'll know exactly where your hard-earned money has gone when you add the totals for the four weeks together by category. If you can do this part of the program, it's a small price to pay for the financial clarity you'll gain from the experience.

I remember working with one male client during his first session. This gentleman already had a sense of the benefits of tracking and had written down all his purchases and expenses for several months. When asked to share them with me, he reached into his briefcase and pulled out a small stack of dingy, curled up Post-it notes that he'd collected over several months. Then it was evident that, like many others, he had skipped a critical step. I asked, "What did the totals tell you about your patterns?" "Well, I didn't add anything up," he replied sheepishly. "I wanted to know where my money was going, but I didn't want to *actually* know how much I was spending."

If you are serious about getting your money straight—after tracking your expenses—you must add them up! It really doesn't count if you don't add up your totals. Without doing that, you may know where your money goes, but you'll be even more enlightened when you see how the small daily amounts add up to a significant monthly figure. Then you can compare it with your spending plan and determine where you overspent and where you underspent. Where did you binge and where were you deprived? What is your comfort level with the amounts? The actual tracking will help you more accurately complete your spending plan for the following month.

Let's refer back to Rachel's monthly spending plan from Chapter Six. Here are the results after she tracked her spending for the month:

Monthly Spending Plan

	Plan	Actual		Plan	Actual
Food			**Recovery/Self-Improvement**		
Groceries	145	121	Spiritual	20	20
Breakfast	10	9	Total	20	20
Lunch	25	43			
Total	180	173	**Dependent Care**		
			Children's Charities	24	24
Shelter			Total	24	24
Mortgage	875	875			
Homeowner's Dues	170	170	**Transportation**		
Phone	30	47	Gas	33	20
Gas and Electric	30	30	Parking/Tolls	1	1
Cable	26	26	Bus	60	30
Newspaper	20	2	Car Wash	4	-
Household Items	20	5	Total	98	51
Insurance	20	20			
Plumbing Repair	-	187	**Entertainment**		
Total	1,191	1,362	Movies	8	-
			Books	30	22
Self-Care			Dance Class	50	-
Clothing	50	-	Total	88	22
Hair Care	100	100			
Medical	30	30			
Dry Cleaners/ Laundry	20	-			
Gym	50	50			
Toiletries	-	3			
Total	250	183			

	Plan	Actual		Plan	Actual
Debt Repayment			**Miscellaneous**		
Sears	20	18	Birthday Gift	20	–
Visa	120	129	Internet	15	15
Macy's	80	84	Total	35	15
Totals	220	231			

	Plan	Actual
Cash on Hand	-340*	-340
Total Expenses	2,106	2,081
Total Income	2,450	2,450
Cash flow	4	29

* Money owed for the previous payroll deposit error

The bottom line is that Rachel came in under plan with $29 cash left over at the end of the month. This was great and a real success for her. With her spending plan and detailed tracking, Rachel was able to meet her needs and tie up loose ends like reimbursing the payroll deposit error, all without going into deprivation.

Rarely will your spending come out exactly as planned. But let's look more closely at Rachel's actual expenses to see how close her estimates were and how she dealt with an unexpected emergency.

- **Food**. Rachel treated herself to eating out for lunch on two unplanned occasions, so she made a conscious choice to spend less for groceries and still came in under plan.

- **Shelter**. Housing expenses are generally pretty fixed costs, except this month the phone bill was higher and an unexpected plumbing problem cost $187. Rachel simply went to her spending plan and made conscious choices to reduce her spending in certain areas—household items, newspaper, clothing, dry cleaning, movies, dance class, and birthday gifts—to cover the expense.

- **Transportation**. Rachel carpooled to work for half of the month and strategically planned her errands to hit all of those in one section of the city on the same day. This way she wouldn't waste gasoline by making several trips each week.

- **Debt Repayment**. Here she chose to use her extra cash flow from carpooling to pay a few extra dollars on two credit cards, which is always good because it helps to reduce the principal balance.

Again, because she had a plan, Rachel didn't panic when an unexpected expense occurred. She knew in advance what her strategy was for the month and knew what bills would be paid from which paycheck. Because she knew exactly what she had spent so far that month, she could make conscious choices and remain in control of her finances instead of letting an unexpected emergency throw her into chaos. In so doing, Rachel maintained power over her money. Her spending plan and monthly tracking gave her all the tools she needed to evaluate her options. She asked herself, "What do I need to do to take care of myself in this situation?" and then she took decisive action.

History Is the Best Teacher

One of the great benefits of tracking your expenses over a long period of time is that you have a history to look back on. Use the Annual Recap of actual expenses on page 171 to help you determine the fluctuations in spending patterns and income that may warrant attention. Over a twelve-month period you may not have noticed how your food expenses gradually increased, but with your tracking as witness, you can make a conscious effort to pull in the reins and regain control. Often clients will bring the previous year's workbook with them to appointments as well as the current year's. Invariably, a question will come up where they can easily refer to the prior year's spending and with confidence make new estimates and financial decisions.

With conscientious tracking, we can identify our weak spots—excessive clothes shopping like Tamika or frequent hairstyle changes like Mattie. If we really get inside our money patterns, we can see where the major "leaks" are. You may discover your own obsession for eating meals out or superfluous travel. Ultimately, tracking can highlight previously overlooked patterns of spending that can wreak havoc on your finances. The tracking doesn't lie. You should be prepared for some mistakes—but don't panic if for the first couple of months you overspend in some areas. This is just the first step to seeing where you need to be more careful in the future. Strive for progress, not perfection. And know that tracking is a real key to breaking financially destructive habits.

Annual Recap _____ Year

	Jan. actual	Feb. actual	March actual	April actual	May actual	June actual	July actual	Aug. actual	Sept. actual	Oct. actual	Nov. actual	Dec. actual	Annual Total
Food													
Shelter													
Self-Care													
Recovery													
Dependent Care													
Transportation													
Entertainment													
Investments													
Monthly Allocations													
Miscellaneous													
Debt Repayment													
One-Time Expenses													
Total Expenses													
Total Income													
Cash on Hand +													
Income +													
Total Income =													
Expenses −													
Cash Flow													

Exercise One: Fight Resistance with Reasonable Rewards

Barbara Sher, motivational speaker and author of *I Could Do Anything If Only I Knew What It Was*, says, "Sometimes the only thing we do to avoid success is refuse to be energetic on our own behalf." That refusal to be energetic is better known as resistance. We have all experienced it for one reason or another. One of the biggest areas of resistance that I have to deal with is in sticking to an exercise program. It's been an ongoing struggle for many years. Perhaps because I've been blessed all of my life to not have weight issues, I've not felt pressed to succeed in this area. But as I get older, it's evident that some of my aches, pains, and stress could be avoided if I made myself physically active on a regular basis.

A few years ago, I found that the best way to get myself to exercise was to figure out the right enticement. So I joined a gym that had among its many amenities something I have a great passion for—namely, a steam room. I absolutely love the heat and the moisture, and it's a great place for me to meditate and get grounded. After joining the gym, I was thrilled at the prospect of doing a "steam" at my convenience. But I placed a condition on its usage. I promised myself I would do a steam only if I did an honest workout, such as spending thirty minutes on the stationary bike or treadmill and thirty minutes in the weight room or taking a one-hour aerobics class. The steam was a sweet reward for the resistance I had to overcome to doing any exercise.

If you find yourself being resistant to tracking your spending, consider finding the right enticement. Let's say you agree to the following:

"I, _____, make a commitment to track my spending at the end of each day." At the end of the week, how would you like to reward yourself? What makes you feel good? Think of a nice perk to give to yourself when you keep the promise as well as something to do if you don't keep the promise. For example:

- **Reward.** Buy flowers for your desk at work and enjoy your accomplishment each time you glance at them during the course of the day.
- **Nonreward.** Buy flowers and give them to your least favorite person in the office.

- **Reward.** Treat yourself to a manicure and reflect on your accomplishment each time you view the beauty of your nails.
- **Nonreward.** Make a $10 contribution to the favorite charity of a coworker.

- **Reward.** Park your car in the company parking lot during the following week.
- **Nonreward.** Park your car three blocks away from your office, and as you walk to work, contemplate how good it will feel knowing where your money goes when you track consistently.

Make a list of ten rewards that motivate you to keep your commitment and ten nonrewards that you'd rather avoid. Keep in mind that the things you choose don't have to cost money. For example, a reward might be to use the dishwasher to clean the dinner dishes and the nonreward is to hand-wash the dishes for one week. Another one of my favorites is to limit myself to a five-minute shower daily compared to a nice, long hot shower to start the day.

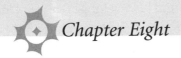

Chapter Eight

Prescription 5: Pay Off Debt with Discipline— Not Deprivation

How many of you would like to be debt free?

This is a question I ask the audience in practically every seminar I teach. Invariably, every person in the room will raise a hand and a ripple of nervous laughter will follow as they remember gorging on clothes, shoes, hair, nails, restaurants, travel, household goods, electronics, appliances, and so on. You name it, we've bought it, and then we wondered where all of our money went or questioned why we have so much debt. According to the Federal Reserve Board, consumer debt exceeded $1.2 trillion dollars in 1996 and has been climbing every year since 1993.

Many of our purchases are unavoidable. As we mentioned in Chapter Six, food, clothing, shelter, and other basic needs must be covered. But some of our other purchases fall into the category of indulgence. If we find ourselves buying, buying, and buying long after we've satisfied our requirements for survival, it may be that we are shopping not out of necessity but out of compulsion. And compulsive shopping is the fastest way to rack up debt that can destabilize our finances, our credit, and create even more trouble down the road.

Are You a Compulsive Shopper?

Are you a compulsive debtor and spender? Take a blank sheet of paper and number it from one to sixteen down the left-hand margin. Now answer the following questions truthfully, marking a yes or no on your paper beside each question:

- Do you like to be seen wearing a different outfit every day?
- Are all of your credit cards at the limit?
- Does worry over debts keep you awake at night or interfere with your work?
- Are you dodging calls from creditors or people to whom you owe money?
- Do you feel inadequate because you've run up debt?
- The last time you used your credit card to purchase something, were you unsure about where you'd get the money to pay it back?
- Do you get cash on your credit card to pay for rent or food?
- Are you afraid to balance your checkbook, tally up how much you owe, or learn the amount of interest you pay on loans?
- Do you drink, eat, shop, or get high to forget money problems?
- Do you always come home with a shopping bag of so-called bargains?
- Do you spend now, believing you'll save when your "big break" comes?

- Do you often borrow money from friends or relatives, or from both?
- Do you buy more food than you or your family eats or needs, or buy too little food so you can pay creditors?
- Do you leave packages in the car to avoid having to justify purchases to your spouse or partner?
- Do you keep secrets from your spouse or partner about debts?
- Are you too proud to seek professional help even when your family's stability is threatened by your mismanagement?

If you answered yes to seven or more of these questions, you probably are a compulsive debtor and spender. Constantly thinking about shopping, and acting on those urges even though it damages your relationships and keeps you in debt, is a clear indication of a compulsive shopping disorder.

I think most of us would agree that shopping has become the Great American Pastime. Often we use our lunch breaks to browse in the stores, stop off after work to check out the sales racks, or at the slightest sign of boredom go out and cruise the shopping centers under the premise that we're "just looking." One woman I know proudly calls herself a "mall mom" and entertains herself and kids by frequenting the shopping malls on weekends. And watch out if there's an outlet mall nearby! We'll occupy ourselves intently in the search for those elusive bargains.

But that's not all. With a bombardment of catalogues, television home shopping networks, and convenient online shopping, we can sit at home in our bathrobes or in our offices at work and shop 'til we drop. We don't even have to leave home to get groceries anymore. Even they can be ordered over the Web! With shopping becoming so easy, it's not hard to overspend. Feelings of dissatisfaction with our lives can cause an urge to splurge; social pressures to keep up with the Joneses have us constantly competing; media advertising has become more clever and persuasive, and hardly realizing it, more and more of us find ourselves deep in debt and searching for ways to get out. In 1999, bankruptcy filings were at 1.25 million. It's an unfortunate statistic demonstrating the pattern of how many of us overextend ourselves with credit.

Credit As a Financial Tool

Technically, there is absolutely nothing wrong with having credit. That statement may surprise you coming from me, a financial recovery expert. But it's true. Credit is a necessary part of the economy. If you want to borrow money for major purchases like a home or car—and most of us have to because we don't have access to large sums of cash—you have to have credit to show a history of timely repayment. So credit itself isn't the problem, and in fact it can be extremely helpful if we use it wisely. It's the *abuse* of credit that gets us into trouble. So what constitutes abuse? Excessive outstanding debt. Too many IOUs. "In its simplest definition," says Jerrold Mundis, author of *How to Get Out of Debt, Stay Out of Debt and Live Prosperously,* "you are in debt when you owe some person or institution money."

There are two different kinds of debt. Many consider secured loans to be "good" debt. A loan is secured if something of equal or greater value is held by the lender as collateral until the loan is repaid. For instance, common types of collateral are cars, homes, savings accounts, and boats. Other types include life insurance policies with a cash value, 401K funds, stocks and bonds, land, and inventory; even a business can be used for security. The idea is that if need be, you can sell the house, car, boat, or business to pay off the loan. Or you can simply forfeit the collateral (in the case of a savings account or life insurance) and have no further obligation. That's why for our purposes we don't view secured loans as debt. Even though money has been lent to you, you can forfeit at any time and be debt free.

Unsecured debt might be considered bad debt. This refers to cash borrowed, credit extended, and services received where nothing is provided to support the loan. These things aren't bad in and of themselves—what's bad and potentially dangerous is outstanding debt that has no supporting collateral and can't be repaid over a three-month period. It can easily turn into long-term debt that takes years to pay off, at high interest rates.

"It is ironic that so many of us are in debt, when culturally, we African Americans have a strong bias against owing others money," says Pamela Ayo Yetunde, author of *Beyond 40 Acres and Another Pair of Shoes.* "Our culture was to pay cash for what we wanted and needed. We used to pay outright, and when we did not have the money, we did not get the desired object (or we put it on layaway). Our culture has gone from paying cash outright to paying nothing, in large part because financial institutions introduced credit cards to the financially vulnerable and immature in our communities." This is noticeably true in the case of college students with no source of income and low- or fixed-income individuals who are already overextended with credit.

Banks will take a risk lending to these people because profits from good accounts more than offset losses. They are well aware that most folks will do whatever they can to at least make the minimum payments to avoid hurting their credit reports. For banks, it's all about making money. In a 1996 article called "The Borrowing Binge" in the *San Francisco Examiner,* William Keenan, senior vice president of marketing at the credit-card unit of Natwest Bank, is quoted as saying, "You cannot make money lending to people who won't pay back, but you can make money lending to people who might have trouble paying back."

Addicted to Debt

After my financial and life crises, I didn't have access to any credit cards. I functioned on a cash basis and paid in advance when needing to do things like reserve a hotel room. I even traveled to Mexico without using a credit card. By doing so, I changed my life and learned to live within my means. About five years later, I obtained a credit card, and for the first couple of months I put no charges on the account and essentially forgot I had it. But on the first weekend that I didn't have the cash for concert tickets, my thoughts immediately went to the credit card. Temptation was staring me in the face, and an overwhelming urge was eating away at my gut to use the card "just this once," know-ing it would trigger the old, familiar addictive pattern.

For many years I didn't accept the idea that compulsive debting and spending was a "disease" as promoted by Debtors Anonymous, a 12-Step program based on the format of Alcoholics Anonymous and designed for people with debt and spending problems. (Check the White Pages for a local telephone number or contact the national office at 781-453-2743.) Mark Bryan and Julia Cameron, authors of *Money Drunk*, describe their former addictive relationships with money as having "an element of hype that both of us found toxic." They go on to explain: "A money addiction might present the same addictive patterns as an addiction to any mood-altering chemical and yield to the same treatment of awareness, acceptance, and action. These money behaviors make sudden sense viewed in terms of a binge cycle: tension, spending, relief, remorse, a period of abstinence or con-trol, then tension, and the cycle begins again."

It's believed that 5 percent of the population suffers from com-pulsive shopping problems. Today, the psychiatric community is look-ing at this syndrome more seriously, believing that these individuals suffer from a type of impulse-control disorder. Professor Lorrin Koran of Stanford University is currently conducting an eight-month study with compulsive shoppers and researching whether the drug serotonin can reduce the urge to shop by correcting a chemical imbalance in the brain. We may be years away from conclusive evidence and widespread acceptance that this chemical imbalance exists, then receiving FDA approval to market the drug. In the meantime, we must not use this as an excuse for our unhealthy behaviors. Even plastic surgery—cutting up the credit cards—is not enough. We need to change our mind-set to consistently live within our means and not let debt become a source of income or a means of supplementing our income when we covet more than we can afford.

How Darmita Kicked the Spending Habit

Although it took my client, Darmita, five years to actually schedule an appointment to start financial counseling, no one in my ten years in business moved faster or accomplished more than she did once she committed to my program. In only sixteen months, she liquidated $65,000 worth of old medical, dental, income tax, and credit-card bills along with the balloon payment for a second mortgage on her income property. Here's her story:

After living a full year on credit cards when her business stagnated, Darmita became more and more fearful of her enormously accumulating debt. Thankfully, by the end of 1997 she landed an ideal job that paid her an $80,000-a-year salary. It took her five months to get current on her rent and utility payments, but even then the Consumer Credit Counseling Service, a nonprofit debt-management program, recommended that she file for bankruptcy because the $65,000 worth of debt was out of control and seemingly impossible to liquidate.

Darmita consulted a bankruptcy attorney and began the process. Then she decided to meet with me to see if there were any other options. After she laid bare all of her financial wreckage, I commended her for being incredibly courageous: first of all, to show up for the appointment, and second, for being willing to face up to her responsibility. I assured her that if she was serious about wanting help, ready to do the work, and patient with herself and the process, we could accomplish her goal of being debt free by January 2000—the dawn of the new century.

I certainly don't have a crystal ball, but I knew Darmita had strong faith and between her job income (which had the potential for bonuses) and the previous marketing-consultant business that she now did part-time, she had the financial resources to make it happen. I also knew that if she could increase the average $500 per month revenues from her business to $1,000, the money could be applied directly to debt repayment. Additionally, if she curbed her appetite for clothes and entertainment, we could make it happen within her time frame.

Darmita's Turning Point

Darmita started the program, as everyone does, by developing spending plans, tracking her expenditures, and being accountable to check in with me each month to discuss financially related feelings and emotions along with her actual monetary results. During our second session, Darmita experienced a major turning point. In referring to $500 that had come in from the consulting business, she said, "This is my extra money for the month. I always use this income for my 'fun' money." At that moment, without criticism and judgment I simply said, "That's really not your money, because you still have $65,000 worth of debt." I didn't make anything of it at the time because we went right on to other things, but Darmita later told me that it was at that point that reality truly set in—if she didn't get serious about paying her obligations, she'd never reach her full potential. The denial and shame that she carried regarding this financial burden would continue to block abundance from coming into her life. These emotions blocked her from *believing* she could be prosperous. That's when she really made up her mind that she was serious about getting rid of the debt and ready to do whatever it took.

Darmita got busy doing the things necessary to generate more revenue—telephone calls, networking, and asking for business. Miraculously, with her efforts and with God's grace, her consulting income went from $500 one month to $4,000 the next and $5,000 the month after that! She was rolling, and I was as proud as a peacock. Then things slowed down to $2,000 and ultimately $100, and her fear and doubt began to surface again. I encouraged her to not panic, to continue doing the things that were necessary to market herself, and to practice the spiritual principles of prayer, meditation, visualization, and affirmation. After Darmita's daily ritual of praying and meditating, she'd soak in her bathtub and visualize an abundant lifestyle—free of debt and financial worries. She saw herself enjoying life with good credit and no bill collectors calling. She also created the affirmation "I am debt free. Money flows to me through all areas of my life—enough to spare and to share." Within no time at all her business income went back up to $5,000, then $10,000 twice, and finally $6,000. By that time, sixteen months after our first session, all of her debts had been paid off. Even more amazing was that the debts could have been paid off in about twelve months. But Darmita chose to not deprive herself too much. She modified her eating-out patterns and kept her clothing and footwear purchases to a minimum. But during this sixteen-month period she maintained fun in her life, continuing her tradition of an annual Christmas party and periodic getaway trips.

Once Darmita made up her mind to get serious, she did the internal work that effected the external changes she desired. But in order to get even that far, she had to embrace a powerful mental habit of abundance—namely, to come clean and face her financial wreckage with honesty and integrity. Until we make this practice a fundamental part of our lives, we'll continue to block the abundance and prosperity that can improve not only our net worth but our self-worth as well.

These results are extraordinary. I grant you that. But I've come to realize that it's all relative. Deep inside, Darmita believed she had the ability to have financial harmony in her life. The income numbers didn't frighten her as much as her high accumulated debt. Some people start to panic when their debt hits $10,000. Others feel it's manageable until it goes over $30,000. When you've exceeded your debt comfort level and fear sets in, use the following statement, as I did on the many occasions when waves of anxiety would overwhelm me during my financial crisis. I would stand in front of the mirror, look myself in the eye, and repeat this statement over and over with as much conviction as I could muster: *Countless others have already freed themselves from debt. I am just the same as them. I can do it too. I AM doing it. I am doing it NOW.*

College Students and Debt

Many college students are book smart but lack the financial savvy to manage money wisely. Like many of us adults, they start out with the misconception that credit-card limits are more like a balance to be drawn against than a loan that has to be repaid. They think of credit as an asset rather than the liability that it really is and are caught up in the mind-set "spend now and worry later" because somehow it isn't real money.

Students don't always realize that though their student loan payments can be deferred until after graduation, credit-card obligations have to be dealt with immediately. Sometimes parents break down and bail out their sons or daughters, usually after a stern conversation about the ills of credit abuse. At other times, students end up dropping out of school to get jobs so they can pay off the debt created by living large on credit cards.

At age twenty-five, Yolanda seemed to have it all: a freshly minted master's degree from New York University and a new job as a marketing coordinator with a San Francisco corporation. But as she put it, "The big glaring eyesore in this otherwise perfect picture is the $37,000 in student loans and the $15,000 in credit-card debt that I accumulated along the way." With the high cost of education, Yolanda's student loan debt wasn't too surprising. But the credit-card debt left over from her freewheeling college days—when car rentals, gift purchases, and airline tickets were hers for the charging—seriously cut into her cash flow, forcing her to live with her family. "Money represents a measure of independence to me," she said, "yet given my current financial situation, I can't even afford to move out and get a place of my own."

Banks and credit-card companies consider today's college students tomorrow's high-income earners. Companies mount major campaigns for student business, sending preapproved cards in the mail, offering free gifts, and setting up tables and displays in student unions and even right outside classrooms! They approve credit cards with limits ranging from $500 to $2,000 when the applicant simply submits a photocopy of current student registration—no verification of income necessary. Companies know these students will want higher credit lines, car loans, home loans, and other financial services in the future, so they hook students into credit relationships as early as their freshman year.

What Should Recent Grads Do?

For Yolanda, beginning a new career with a $32,000 annual income and $52,000 in debt is a horrendous burden. What advice would I give to Yolanda and other students for dealing with postgraduation indebtedness?

Communicate with your lenders.
Inquire about all possible options, including:

- *Deferred repayment programs.* In addition to a six-month grace period after graduation, you may qualify for federal student loan deferments, which can be granted for such reasons as continuing your education or even unemployment. Interest may or may not accrue during this period, depending on your type of loan.

- *Forbearance.* This time-out from paying back a loan is granted at the lender's discretion, but be aware that interest continues to accrue.

- *Consolidating loans.* Combining several loans into one payment can help lower your monthly payment. The Federal Direct Consolidation Loan program may allow you to consolidate federal loans with various repayment options. Call 1-800-848-0982 for information.

Control spending.
Develop a monthly spending plan. Track your expenses and analyze where your money goes. Look for any areas of impulse buying and redirect those dollars to debt repayment.

Pay off credit cards and high-interest-rate loans first.
Eliminating these debts will save you money in the long run, because more of your hard-earned dollars will be applied to the principal (the actual amount of money you borrowed versus interest payments). To avoid the temptation to create additional debt, close the credit-card accounts. Even though accounts may carry balances, they can still be closed—you just won't be able to make new charges. Continue making your payments, and if you feel the need, keep one major credit card open for emergencies.

Double up payments on student loans.
After eliminating the credit-card debt, use those funds to increase payments on student loan debt.

The Quick Fix: Loan Consolidations

At the point where we start to feel overwhelmed and panicky about our accumulated debt, we naturally look for ways to relieve the pressure. True to human nature, we look for the quick fix—often going back to the sources that helped us get into financial trouble. The consolidation loan is a good tool to use, but unless you've dealt with the reasons *why* you created the problem in the first place, the relief will probably be temporary. Such loans make a lot of sense and have become quite popular over the last twenty years. According to Knight Credit Card Services, the average family who is in credit-card debt carries a balance of $4,000 on several cards from month to month, and the average number of credit cards per household is ten. If you are reading this book, you may or may not be above average, as many of my clients are. But let's consider the following as an example of where you might be:

Your Card	Your Balance	Minimum Payment	Interest Rate
Visa	$5,000	$100	19.4%
Visa Platinum	$10,000	$200	15.5%
MasterCard	$4,000	$120	18.0%
Target	$1,000	$20	21.0%
Macy's	$2,000	$40	21.6%
Total	$22,000	$480	

With a consolidation loan, instead of making five payments to five different lenders, you would seek to have one lender provide $22,000 to pay off the debt, leaving you with one payment to worry about, preferably with a lower monthly payment and interest rate. One option might be to consolidate onto one credit card by transferring all your balances to that card. Or you could ask your current Visa or MasterCard lender for a credit-line increase. One of my clients, Clara, telephoned one of her creditors to request an increase to $9,000 to consolidate all of her accounts to one card. The customer service representative listened to her request and then said, "No, I'm sorry. We can't do that." Clara hung up the phone, waited five minutes, and then called back. She got another customer service representative, who listened to her request and said, "No, I don't think we can do that." Clara hung up the phone, waited five minutes, and then called back. She got a third customer service representative, who listened to her request and then said, "Okay, I can do that for you." Surprisingly, her tenacity paid off and we both learned a valuable lesson—it never hurts to ask for what you want!

A second option might be to obtain a line of credit from your bank or credit union. This is a revolving account, meaning you are approved up to a specific amount, your monthly payment is based on the balance outstanding, and whatever you repay becomes available for you to borrow again. In other words, the less you owe, the less you have to pay. It is sometimes an unsecured loan, there is no card attached to it, and you access the line either by check, in person, or with a telephone call to the lender.

A third option, the home equity loan, can be a line of credit or a term loan. If it's a term loan, it means you borrow all the money at once, it is not revolving, you make a specific payment each month, and it has a specific payoff date. If you own real estate, you probably want to consider a home equity loan. It is also a second mortgage on your property. The advantage is that in most cases the interest you pay on the loan is tax deductible, as opposed to credit cards, from which the interest can no longer be deducted. Here is an example of how it works:

Appraised value of your home	$100,000
First mortgage	- $55,000
Equity in home	**$45,000**

Banks will typically lend up to 80 percent of the value of the home less the amount of the outstanding mortgage. So in this case, here is what it looks like:

80% of appraised value	$80,000
First mortgage	- $55,000
Available to loan	$25,000
Home equity (consolidation loan)	- $22,000
Remaining equity in home	**$3,000**

In this case, the bank has given you $22,000 to apply to your other debts, while $3,000 remains in your home. Again, the advantage of this loan is that it reduces the payments from five to one—you no longer need to worry about paying off Visa or Target; you simply need to make your monthly payment to the bank. Furthermore, with a fifteen-year home equity term loan your interest rate would be lowered to about 9.6 percent and the monthly payment would be approximately $231 per month. If you decided to go with a home equity line of credit, the estimated interest rate would be 8 percent with a $308 monthly payment and would take just over eight years to pay off, assuming the interest rate didn't change and you didn't advance any additional money.

Refinancing Your First Mortgage

Another option in loan consolidation is to refinance your first mortgage to include the credit-card payoff in the new loan. For example, let's again say that the appraised value of your home is $100,000 and a bank is willing to lend up to 80 percent of that amount, or $80,000. In this case, the bank would pay off your $22,000 credit-card balances, pay off the existing mortgage of $55,000, and make you a new loan of $77,000.

Appraised value of the home	$100,000	
80% of appraised value of home	$80,000	
New first mortgage	$77,000	($55K mortgage +
		$22K credit cards)
Remaining equity	**$3,000**	

The new first mortgage would have an approximate 7.75 percent interest rate, a thirty-year term, and a monthly payment of $551.64. Keep in mind that although you now have only one payment to make, it also means you have stretched the payoff of the $22,000 credit-card balance to thirty years as well as the former $55,000 mortgage, which may have had only twenty years to go.

Some lenders will lend 100 or 125 percent of the appraised value of your home. But be cautious of these programs. They usually charge an exceptionally high interest rate because of the risk. They know that if you default on the loan, they can foreclose on your home. Just as with the credit cards mentioned earlier in the chapter, these lending institutions know they can profit from your struggle to make the high payments because you won't want to lose your home.

By the way, consider setting up your new or current mortgage for biweekly payments instead of once a month. This can significantly lower the amount of interest you'll pay over the life of the loan. For example, a $77,000 mortgage with a monthly payment of $551.64 for thirty years means you would pay $198,590.40—or $121,590.40 in interest alone. If you make biweekly payments of $275.82, you would pay the same loan off in approximately twenty-three years and spend only $88,300 in interest! A savings of $33,290.40! This happens because you pay interest on the principal balance and for twenty-three years you've made one half of your payment fifteen days early, which accelerates reduction of the outstanding balance. Some lenders charge a small fee of about $300 to set up this arrangement, but it's worth it because of the thousands of dollars you save in the long run.

If your lender does not have this payment option available, try to make at least one extra mortgage payment per year. You won't garner the same type of savings, but over time you will still come out ahead.

Consumer Credit Counselors: Another Type of Consolidation

As mentioned previously, the Consumer Credit Counseling Service is a nonprofit debt-management program that allows you to lower your credit-card interest rates to zero, in some cases, and to cut your monthly payments without filing for bankruptcy. If accepted into the CCCS program, you make one payment monthly to CCCS, which distributes the agreed-upon amounts to your various creditors for a small fee. It is a structured program that has worked for many individuals and couples. I highly recommend it, although it doesn't provide the same amount of financial empowerment as when you accept the responsibility to pay creditors yourself. It also appears on the credit report and can be viewed as a red flag to lenders.

Bankruptcy—The Ultimate Quick Fix

Americans in epidemic numbers use credit cards and lines of credit to live beyond their means, as evidenced by the all-time-high personal bankruptcy filings in 1998, which exceeded 1.4 million. Bankruptcy is a legal procedure that eliminates debt owed to creditors. There are two common types of bankruptcy filings available to individuals. Chapter 7 is a liquidation bankruptcy, where you give up all your nonexempt assets in exchange for a discharge of all your debts except income taxes owed within three years of the filing date. (Exempt assets include household goods, personal belongings, and possibly your home.) Under Chapter 13 you propose a three-to-five-year repayment plan to the creditors by offering to pay off all or part of the debt from your future income.

Normally, I don't recommend that people file for bankruptcy. Most bankruptcy filings stay on your credit report for seven to ten years. Although there is life after bankruptcy and you can reestablish yourself, it's possible to avoid that severe a blemish on your credit report by getting on track financially in a similar time frame. Another reason to avoid bankruptcy is that if you have asked a friend or relative to cosign a loan, your cosigner will be stuck with your debt.

However, if you chose to file bankruptcy and get a fresh start, it's even more important to follow the steps outlined in this book so you can keep your money straight from that point forward. You won't want to have to exercise that option again, even though legally you can do so after a six-year period.

Credit Reports

Now more than ever, credit reports have become an intricate part of our lives. They are used not only to determine our ability to get credit, but are often required for employment applications, job contracts, insurance policies, and even apartment rentals. Their importance has become so prominent that for many of us it has mistakenly come to define our identity and determine our self-worth. If you are among this group, remember: You are not your credit report! It is simply a reflection of your payment habits over a specified time period.

If your ego is deflated right now because of your credit report, don't worry about it or how you need to rebuild your credit. Let's do first things first and clean it up before you have a need to borrow. Develop your monthly spending plan and follow it. Start paying your bills on time, and most of the information on the report will take care of itself. After you have stabilized your spending by properly planning and tracking monthly, you will begin to see the light at the end of the tunnel. This is the time to walk through the fear and order your credit report. At this point, you want only to see what is there and check it for accuracy. Reports can be ordered from:

Equifax, P.O. Box 740241, Atlanta, GA 30374; call (800) 685-1111; or visit www.equifax.com on the Web.

Experian, P.O. Box 949, Allen, TX 75013; call (888) 397-3742; or visit www.experian.com on the Web.

Trans Union; call (800) 888-4213; or visit www.transunion.com on the Web.

Once you've received your credit report in the mail, you will likely be quite anxious and apprehensive about what it will say. Let's do a ritual before opening the envelope. To prepare for your five-minute meditation, light a scented candle, get into a relaxed position, close your eyes, and begin to concentrate on your breathing. With each slow inhalation, say to yourself, "I breathe in courage and strength," and with each exhalation say, "I breathe out fear and anxiety." Repeat each statement at least ten times. And as you read the report, know that this is a reflection of your past and "the past is not a precedent." You do not have to accept this as your future behavior.

"Seventy percent of adult Americans have some type of derogatory information in their credit histories," notes Bob Hammond, author of *Repair Your Own Credit.* "Because we all know it's in our interest to erase that information, we're susceptible to whatever promises so-called credit experts are willing to make." So beware of any company that charges an up-front fee of several hundred dollars to "clean up" your credit report or "repair" your credit. No one can do more to fix your credit report than you can do for yourself.

After reviewing your report, complete the enclosed form to correct disputed errors and erase outdated information. In the case of disputes, usually the credit bureau will temporarily remove an item while it investigates the claim. But if the item turns out to be accurate, it will go right back on your credit report. Do your best to clear off the negative information and then let it go. Also, ask your creditor to "re-age" your account. This basically brings the account to current status. Don't be afraid to contact the customer service or collection department to make the request. Sometimes clerks don't have the authority, so if you feel you're not getting anywhere, ask for a supervisor.

I remember being stressed out for months because I couldn't find a way to get rid of a car loan for $16,000 that had three thirty-day late payments on the report from only one of the three credit bureaus. I had done an awesome job of paying off accounts, cleaning up my report, and maintaining only two small credit cards. The car loan had been paid off for four or five years, but with this particular bureau, the payment history would remain for seven years. It was one loose end I couldn't get rid of.

Soon after that, my thirteen-year-old car finally died and I attempted to lease a new vehicle. The dealer ran a credit report that showed my credit was clean, but it didn't indicate that I had been extended any credit over a few thousand dollars. Suddenly, I remembered the other credit bureau that had the old car loan on it. The dealer ran the report, verified that I had previously had a car loan, and the next day I drove away in a new Mazda Miata! In this case, the detailed history on my report worked to my advantage. But it just goes to show that bad credit or even no credit can be a problem in obtaining loans and financing your future. Once you have paid off your debt and cleaned up your credit report, the next step is rebuilding your credit.

Rebuilding Your Credit

As stated earlier, a key ingredient to reestablishing your credit is to live within your means and pay bills on time. Since you have already reviewed your credit report for accuracy and corrected the errors and outdated information, here are a few more things you can do:

- *Get credit in your own name.* Even if you are married, it's good to establish a credit report in your own name in case things change. Also, if financial problems are due to your spouse's behavior, you can protect your personal credit rating.

- *Obtain department store or gasoline accounts.* Many of these companies tend to be a bit more lenient regarding blemishes on your credit report. Don't overextend yourself, but it's a good way to get started again with a minimal number of purchases.

- *Take out a secured personal loan.* If you deposit money into a savings account, it can be used as collateral against a personal loan from your bank for the same amount. For example, a savings account for $1,000 entitles you to a personal loan for the same amount with payments of approximately $86.86 for twelve months at 7.25 percent interest. Note that the interest rate on a secured loan is usually lower than that on a regular loan.

- *Obtain a secured credit card.* Many banks offer credit cards where if you deposit funds into an account with them, you can receive a credit card for a similar amount. For example, if you deposit $1,000, you'll receive a credit card with a limit of $1,000. The savings will earn interest while you rebuild a positive credit history with timely payments.

The Ten Do's and Don't's of Becoming Debt Free

Now that we've talked about paying off debt with discipline but without deprivation, read through the following strategies, which will help you stay on track. Decide which ones will work for you, and check them off as you take appropriate action.

- Don't create any new, unnecessary debt. Debt puts you in the hole, so stop digging yourself in deeper. Make a personal commitment to yourself each morning: "I will not create any new debt today." Remember, you can't borrow your way out of debt! Post a calendar where you can easily see it and place a big red heart in the box for each day you keep your commitment. It's a visible sign of how you are loving yourself by not getting any deeper in debt.

- Do close extra charge accounts. You need only one or two credit cards, and the more cards you have, the greater the temptation. Furthermore, having too many accounts open tends to lower your credit score when applying for loans.

- Do use a debit card or check card. Formerly known as the ATM card, at most banks it now has a Visa or MasterCard symbol on it, allowing merchants to accept it like a credit card. The important difference is that you don't incur any debt because the money is immediately deducted from your checking account. You can use it to make purchases or to hold reservations such as with hotels. Keep track of those expenditures in your check register. The debit card is only as good as the amount of money you have in your checking account.

- Don't carry credit cards with you. Contrary to the popular advertising slogan, DO leave home without them! Consider freezing them in a plastic bag with water. If the temptation hits you to use the card, by the time you drive home and thaw out the bag, you will have changed your mind about the purchase. And for goodness' sake, don't cheat by memorizing the account number!

- Don't charge anything that will be gone by the time the bill comes. The reality of one client's deteriorating financial situation finally set in when her husband reported they had sunk so low that they had to finance a loaf of bread. Don't charge meals, movie tickets, or groceries unless you pay off the balance every month.

- Don't be seduced by special offers. Airline miles are not worth it if you're paying finance charges each month because you carry over balances. In many cases, you could have paid for a ticket several times over based on the accumulated finance charges added to the account. Skip-a-payment offers are also a disadvantage to you, because the creditor will charge you interest for the month anyway and that increases your balance.

- Do shift debt to lower-interest-rate cards. Ask your lender to lower the interest rate on your existing accounts. If they refuse, transfer the balance to a new creditor with a lower rate. Go to www.quicken.com or www.bankrate.com on the Internet for information on banks offering lower interest rates.

- Do communicate with creditors. Don't avoid telephone calls or hide from bill collectors. It creates unnecessary shame that can block you from moving forward in your life. And don't make promises you cannot keep. Use the spending plan to determine the appropriate payment, and do it consistently.

- Do make settlement offers to creditors. For past-due debt, negotiate a settlement offer of 50 cents on the dollar with the creditor. For example, if you have a debt of $2,000 that has been outstanding for six months, offer the creditor a $1,000 lump sum to get rid of the debt. It's often more attractive to the creditor to receive the $1,000 than to get a payment of $20 per month for the next five years. Also, ask for immediate removal from the credit report as part of the deal.

- Do get support. Seek financial counseling. Contact the national office of Debtors Anonymous at (781) 453-2743, Credit Counseling Centers, Inc., at (800) 388-2227, or a financial consultant (see the Yellow Pages or Internet).

Exercise One: Finding Your Motivation

Establish a reason why you want to become debt free and find your motivation. What do you keep postponing because you don't have the money? Home improvements? A vehicle? Wouldn't it be motivating to be able to afford a car so you and your children no longer have to wait for the bus in bad weather? It would certainly relieve a lot of pressure to know that your credit card had a zero balance in case you needed to make a sudden trip across the country for a family medical emergency or to attend a funeral. Write down the motivation you've decided on and post it where you can see it every day.

Exercise Two: Establishing Your Targets

When do you want to be debt free? By the year 2002? Pick a target date, a time to shoot for. Be specific and be reasonable. Write the date down next to your motivation. Remember to maintain flexibility and know that you are not a bad person if you have to adjust the timing. Here are some things you can do to meet your target date:

- Sell assets if necessary. Have a garage sale or place items on consignment and use the proceeds to pay down your debt.

- Increase minimum credit-card payments. If you pay only the minimum due, you are mostly paying interest. Add to your minimum payment, even if it's only $10 per month. If only the minimum payment is made, a debt of $5,000 at 18 percent will take twenty-two years to pay off, with $6,923 going to finance charges. Adding $10 per month to that minimum payment would pay off the same debt in 4.5 years, with a total of $2,365 going to finance charges.

- Refer to the basic minimum spending plan that you created in Chapter Six. Keep in mind that this is the plan that details the minimum amount of money you can get by on during any given month. Now add the totals from all the categories in the plan *except* for debt repayment. Finally, subtract that amount from your net income figure. The resulting sum equals the amount of money you have available that can be applied to your debts. For example, let's say that your net income is $2,500 and you have expenses *without* debt payments that come to $1,500. After taking care of all your basic necessities, the amount of available cash left over that can be used to pay down your debt is $1,000. Hopefully, this figure exceeds your minimum debt payments. If not, after reexploring the ways to increase your income from Chapter Six, you may need to review your tracking worksheets to see where additional expenses can be cut back—then revise your basic minimum spending plan.

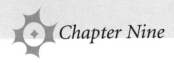

Chapter Nine

Prescription 6: Save Consistently Without Being a Miser

African Americans as a people are actually very familiar with the concept of savings. Whether it involves using a jar, a coffee can, or stuffing money into a mattress, there's a history of saving we can draw upon. In the nineteenth century, after slavery was abolished, some of our ancestors were able to save up enough money to buy land and sustain a family. I'm still amazed that a former slave could save an amount like $500 for land when they had so little to work with. Later in the 1870s, some of our ancestors used the Freedman's Savings and Trust Company, which was founded to help blacks save money and build economic stability. Even back then the bank grew to have thirty-four branches in various states and deposits of over $3 million—accumulated savings from hard work that we should all admire.

Nowadays, some of us have bought into a prosperity myth. On January 1 of any given year, you can pretty much count on finding black-eyed peas cooking in the kitchens of black families across America. In a tradition that is passed from generation to generation, the peas are said to bring good luck, money, and prosperity for the new year. Maybe in a sense it has worked. Many African Americans have prospered in the last ten years given that our buying power as a group is projected to exceed $533 billion in 2000. Again, that's a 70 percent increase over the last decade.

So how are we managing this ever-increasing wealth to make it grow? Ariel Mutual Funds and Charles Schwab & Co., Inc., commissioned the 1999 Black Investors Survey to identify similarities and differences in terms of savings and investment knowledge, attitudes, and behaviors between African Americans and whites with high incomes (household incomes of $50,000 or more). According to the survey, while blacks are underinvested relative to whites, they are actually more interested in investing and financial management. Compared to whites, more African Americans have read books about saving and investing (58 percent vs. 46 percent), gone to an investment seminar (28 percent vs. 22 percent), or joined or participated in an investment club (10 percent vs. 5 percent). But even among this affluent group of African Americans, 41 percent say there is simply no money left over after paying expenses to save and invest.

In 1995, according to the Organization for Economic Cooperation and Development in Washington, D.C., Americans saved on average only 4.7 percent of their disposable income compared to 14.3 percent for the French, 13.4 percent for the Japanese, and 11.6 for the Germans. In 1998, the savings rate in this country dropped to a disturbing .5 percent.

We've Got the Money—So Let's Use It

As you hopefully know by now, it's not that we African American women don't have money. In 1996, more than 300,000 black women (one in twenty-six of the 8.3 million black females in the labor force) earned $50,000 or more. We know how important it is to manage money wisely, because in many cases we're solely responsible for our financial welfare. But heavy debt burdens and excessive spending patterns make many women feel that no matter how much their income may increase over time, they still won't have cash available for large purchases and certainly not for a savings reserve.

Over the years, we may have received positive messages like "If you make a dollar, save a nickel." But we sometimes resist these suggestions for one reason or another. My client Ramona had an uncle who stressed: "If there are two incomes in the family, save the smaller check and live off the larger one." Although the concept registered with Ramona, she always felt she needed both checks to survive and decided to worry about saving and investing later on.

Unfortunately, we also heard less positive messages, such as "if it ain't one thing, it's another." So we grew up expecting something would always prevent us from saving. And, of course, it did! Medical expenses, kid expenses, car repairs, replacing washers, dryers, and refrigerators always came first. Waiting until the end of the month to see what's left to put into savings doesn't work. Usually, there is nothing left, so we promise ourselves we'll try again next month.

Another reason we put off saving money is that we feel we should pay off our debt first and then build a cushion against a "rainy day." The rule of thumb in the financial world is to have three to six months of living expenses set aside in an emergency fund. That figure alone could come to tens of thousands of dollars for some families, and the thought of amassing such an amount only to leave it sitting somewhere in an account can be incredibly frightening and seem totally impractical.

But you *can* pay off your debt and save at the same time. How? By paying yourself first. You can pay yourself a little something even as you pay your bills. That doesn't mean you should build a hefty savings account that earns only 3 percent interest while you're carrying $10,000 in debt at an 18 percent annual interest rate. But putting aside a small stash of just $500 in savings can really add to your peace of mind and help you break the habit of using your credit card for every minor emergency.

How to Start Saving Money

We've all heard and accepted the saying "knowledge is power." Author George Fraser says: "Knowledge is not power. Acting on the knowledge is power." I think there's truth to that too. Our commitment to savings and wealth-building has to become as strong as our commitment to pay our creditors and to pay our taxes. And contrary to what you may think, we don't have to wait for a big chunk of money to get started.

In fact, it's best to open your savings account at a place that is inconvenient to get to so you won't be tempted to make withdrawals. For years I kept a credit union account in another state. That worked for me, because it couldn't get much more inconvenient. And don't keep an ATM card that allows access to the account. Also, delete any overdraft coverage on your checking account that accesses a credit card or savings account. You don't want to accidentally create any new debt or deplete your savings. Here are some additional things you can do to build up the account balance:

Consider yourself a creditor. It's a radical way to think, but you "owe" it to yourself to ensure you make a "payment" to yourself. Take a brightly colored envelope or a plain white envelope decorated to your taste so that it stands out. Write your name on it and the words "Pathway to Prosperity and Wealth" and keep it permanently in the file, box, or basket with your incoming monthly bills. When you write a check to pay the creditor and utilities, write a check to pay yourself too. Use the spending plan you created in Chapter Five to assess your cash flow and start out with a small "bite-sized" amount of $5 or $10. Joyously begin the new habit and be consistent with your payments. The amount per payment can grow later—the important thing is to make a habit of contributing to your savings.

Sign up for payroll deduction with your employer. Have money deducted from your paycheck and deposited in a savings account before you even receive it. We typically adjust our spending to the net income we receive, so this is a good way to coerce yourself to save. Don't start out with too large an amount; otherwise you may be compelled to resort to credit cards to meet your cash flow needs. Adding on debt defeats the purpose and will make you feel like a failure at saving. Start out with a minimum amount of $25 or $50 per check until you've adjusted your spending. That way you won't miss it too much.

Set up an automatic transfer at the bank. With an automatic transfer, a specific amount is withdrawn from your checking account once a month or each pay period and deposited to your savings account. Having the deposits done automatically ensures that contributions to the account will be done consistently. There's virtually no chance of procrastinating in making the deposit and waiting to see if there's money left over at the end of the month. So have the money taken out automatically, forget about it, and be delighted with the savings-account growth when you receive your statement.

Save your spare change. Create a prosperity basket, bottle, or jar to drop your spare change into at the end of the day. Some people use the five-gallon water bottles from home delivery companies to save change. I still put pennies in a bright yellow smiley-face bank that I got when I was sixteen. But I primarily use a little plastic coin roller container that I picked up at the drugstore for $1 that makes it fast and easy to count and roll the coins. You might want to check with the bank in advance to see if they have a coin counter, or if they prefer that you bring your change in loose or prerolled. A dollar a day in spare change doesn't seem like much, but it equals thirty bucks a month that could grow in your savings account. Think of how this simple spare-change concept helped Oprah raise $3,500,000 for her Angel Network Program since its launch in 1997.

Start a "serial savings" plan. Each time you break a large bill, check the serial numbers on the $1 bills you receive in change to see if any of the bills begin with your initials. For example, I look for bills with serial numbers starting with G, F, or B. When I find them, I set them aside in my wallet and at the end of the day put them in an envelope that gets deposited into savings at the end of the month. While reviewing the prior month's spending with one couple recently, I noticed they had planned to save $100 but, in fact, had saved $160. I congratulated them, and the wife replied, "Well, I took your advice about the serial savings plan and found at least two per day with my son's initial on it. That came to $60 for the month, so we increased our savings deposit. My eight-year-old is so excited about the game that he now wants to use $10 bills and $20 bills too. I told him we'll have to work our way up to that, but we're still having fun in the meantime."

Do a "dollar savings" plan. If your cash flow is a little looser, you can use the same principle as above, only set aside all of the $1 bills that you receive or that you have left at the end of the day. It's best to keep an envelope in your purse and put the dollars immediately into it. I did that for the last couple of months of 1999 and was able to accumulate almost $200. Instead of immediately depositing it, I used that as my Y2K emergency money, and when no crisis occurred, I then deposited the money into my account.

Put your expense checks in savings. If you are reimbursed for business expenses, the monthly checks that you receive can be deposited immediately into your savings account.

Deposit at least half of all gift money into savings. If you receive cash as a birthday or holiday gift, put at least half of it into savings and use the other half to get yourself a treat.

Open a Christmas Club or holiday account. This account, which is offered by most banks and credit unions, allows you to make deposits starting in December or January of each year. Moneys are accumulated throughout the year and payable each November—just in time for the holiday season. You're prohibited from making withdrawals during the year without closing the account, so this restriction helps you resist temptation. When the holiday festivities begin, you can spend without pressure because you've been saving all year long for that specific purpose.

Check your motives behind all spending. Assess if each purchase is for immediate gratification or if it has long-term value. If it falls in the immediate gratification category, consider giving up the purchase and depositing the money you were about to spend into your savings instead. Small amounts add up over time, so practice vigilance and consistency.

Long-Term Savings

If it's hard to get sisters to implement a program to build a savings cushion for short-term security, it can be especially difficult to garner funds for long-term planning. After we get past the rainy-day cushion, and pay off our debt, we need to look toward the future and financially plan to support our lifestyle in retirement. It's never too early to start, and even if you have a bit of catching up to do—it's not too late to begin building your long-term security.

An important way to pay yourself first is to take advantage of retirement plans where you work. Be sure to maximize your contributions, especially if your company is willing to match funds. If contributing the maximum feels too scary, start with 5 percent, then increase it next year to 10 percent, and then to the maximum percentage of 15. Remember, because these are pretax dollars, the reduction to your net paycheck will make less of an impact than you think—probably less than 10 percent.

Here's an example: If your gross monthly paycheck is $2,000 and you are in a 15 percent tax bracket, then your net income equals about $1,700 with zero dollars in retirement contribution. If you sign up for the 5 percent contribution and your employer matches it dollar for dollar, then $100 is deducted from your gross income of $2,000 and your taxable income is $1,900. Again, assuming you are in a 15 percent tax bracket, your new net is $1,615. Although you have $85 less in net income, the advantage is that you now have $200 in retirement and you've saved $15 on your taxes. And it just gets better the more you have deducted. Let's look at what happens if you maximize your contributions:

Without contribution	5% contribution + match	15% contribution + match
$2,000 gross income	$2,000 gross income	$2,000 gross income
- 300 15% taxes	- 100 5% contribution	- 300 15% contribution
$1,700 net income	$1,900 taxable income	$1,700 taxable income
	- 285 15% taxes	- 255 15% taxes
	$1,615 net income	$1,455 net income
	$100 5% contribution	$300 15% contribution
	$100 company match	$300 company match
Zero in retirement	$200 total retirement	$600 total retirement
Zero tax savings	$15 tax savings	$45 tax savings

This example doesn't even show the interest or profits you'll earn on the retirement account, but see how easy it is to make your dollars grow! The real payoff is when your employer matches your contributions. You can't afford to miss the opportunity whether the match is 5, 25, or 100 percent. So, familiarize yourself with your employer's plan and its investment options. Know how long it takes to become vested (the point at which you have the right to the entire balance of your account, including the employer's contribution). It usually takes about five years. Here are some specific steps you can take to start saving for the long term:

Join your employer's 401K plan. This employer-sponsored salary-deferral plan allows individuals to contribute a portion of their gross salary to a savings or investment plan or company profit-sharing plan. Contributions and income earned are tax deferred until withdrawn at age 59½, or when the employee retires or leaves the company. Try not to borrow against or withdraw from your 401K or 403(B) (the tax-deferred savings plan for employees of public employers and employees of not-for-profit organizations).

Open an Individual Retirement Account (IRA). This account allows anyone with earned income to contribute to an IRA on a tax-deferred basis. Individuals may contribute up to $2,000 a year (up to $2,250 if an individual has a nonworking spouse), deducting IRA contributions from adjusted gross income in federal tax returns. Interest income on the principal amount accumulates tax free, and account assets are not taxed until withdrawals begin.

Open a Simplified Employee Pension (SEP). The SEP-IRA is a tax-deferred pension plan in which an IRA is funded by employer and employee contributions. Contributions are tax deductible and earnings tax deferred. SEPs are for companies with twenty-five or fewer employees or for self-employed persons. You can contribute a fixed percentage of your earned net income (up to $25,500 in 2000).

Open a Keogh account. This tax-deferred savings plan allows self-employed persons and employees of a business to save money for retirement. Owners of a Keogh make regular or annual contributions, up to 25 percent of net profits or a maximum of $30,000, to a profit-sharing plan or pension plan under a qualified trustee. A Keogh account must be set up by December 31, although contributions for a calendar year may be made at any time before the April 15 filing deadline for federal tax returns.

As mentioned earlier, the most important step in saving is just getting started. Once you've done that, you can focus on increasing the contributions over time. Make a commitment to yourself that you'll continue to live within your means and forward any annual pay raises directly to savings or investments. After allocating a reasonable portion of each month's paycheck to paying yourself, do the same with any bonuses, severance packages, lawsuit and divorce settlements, insurance benefits, inheritances, tax returns, and unexpected windfalls.

Other Ways to Save
Be Nice to Airlines and Be Nice to Yourself. If you have occasion to travel by airplane with any regularity, you probably already know the benefits of joining airline mileage programs. If not, be aware that you

can earn miles for each trip you make toward a free airline ticket or a ticket upgrade. Try to use one airline consistently so that your miles accrue quickly. Even if you don't think you'll be flying much, sign up anyway. It costs you nothing, and who knows what kind of travel you'll attract once you open yourself to the possibilities. There are also partnerships between airlines and certain credit-card companies that record a mile for each dollar purchased on the card. Again, it's a way to accrue free miles, but as we discussed in Chapter Eight, don't get seduced into using the card for the miles unless you pay your balance in full each month. Otherwise, the interest you pay on the card over time will far exceed the cost of the "free" ticket.

Many of us are in a hurry-hurry-rush-rush mode when we travel. But I've found that it can be financially beneficial to slow down and enjoy the moment. If your flight is overbooked, for example, you can volunteer to give up your seat and take a later flight in exchange for significant airline credit. Sometimes the next flight is only an hour or two later, sometimes it's the next morning, in which case you also get overnight hotel accommodations and meals included in the deal. I volunteered twice on a recent trip from California to Detroit—in total receiving a $300 credit, a free meal, and another $25 credit just for offering to wait. During my wait I had an excellent meal, worked on my laptop, had friendly conversations with other travelers, and read a good book. I arrived in Detroit a few hours later than originally planned, but I was well rested and had what amounted to a free ticket across the country again. I'll use the credits to help pay the airfare on my next vacation!

Stay Home and Cocoon. One of the best ways I've found to save money is to not spend money. There's more available to save if I don't "nickel-and-dime" it away. And the best way to make sure of that is to do something very simple. Stay home! That's it. Stay home and enjoy the comfort of your living space. Create an environment that is a sacred space, a precious sanctuary. It may take some work to pull it all together, but it's worth it when the energy is pleasing and peaceful in your home. Many of us have become pack rats over the years; we have so much "stuff" that it diverts our attention, zaps our energy, and prevents us from relaxing in our living space. Two great books to read on dealing with the stuff in our physical, mental, and emotional space are *Clear Your Clutter with Feng Shui* and *Creating Sacred Space with Feng Shui* by Karen Kingston. The night I started reading the book on clutter, I got so motivated that I couldn't go to sleep until two A.M. and was up out of bed at seven A.M., implementing her suggestions. Another client of mine, who was very familiar with feng shui, the Chinese art of arranging possessions to make the home harmonious and prosperous, was so excited that she immediately went out and bought four copies of the book to give to her best friends.

When your home is a place where you are at peace and enjoy spending time, there's less of a desire to leave it to spend more money. Start a collection of videotapes of television programs that move and inspire you. When I want to laugh, I rewatch the celebration honoring Richard Pryor that was hosted by Eddie Murphy. When I want to feel hometown pride, I rewatch *Motown 40*. During my special time at home, I'll listen to jazz or gospel, or go to my collection of "feel-good" movies, and will be well entertained for free.

Along the same lines, getting together with friends doesn't always have to be a food-focused activity like going out to lunch or dinner. We also don't have to be the first to see movies when they come out. What's the advantage of having the premium cable channels if you've seen all the movies that are aired? Taking a nice walk by the marina or lake, through the neighborhood, to the park, or along the walking trail gives us a chance to chat and is good exercise too. Or we may choose to stay home, have a glass of wine or juice, and enjoy one another's company.

Don't be afraid just to be with yourself for a while. Make a commitment to unplug the television, radio, and telephone for one evening per week for a month. (If you must, you can check for phone messages midway through the evening and deal only with emergencies.) Use the time to write down your thoughts, feelings, and desires in a journal. Clear the clutter from your mind and begin to focus on what you want to accomplish. Make the connection of how saving and investing can help you reach your goal. Use this quiet time to internalize the message and commit to the strategies.

Exercise One: Make Work Work for You

In many cases, businesses offer their employees a variety of ways to gain knowledge about financial matters and help them save easily for their futures. Here are a few things you can do to become more financially empowered:

- **Make an appointment with the plan administrator** at work to clarify any questions about the retirement program. There is nothing more shocking than finding out that the retirement plan you were banking on is not what you expected it to be. Make sure you understand fully what its terms and conditions are.

- **Attend all financial seminars** offered at work. There may be programs and policies that you don't know about that can materially increase your financial health.

- **Check with your former employers** and verify if any 401K funds are due you. If they are, you may need to ask a financial adviser about the best way to reinvest such funds.

Exercise Two: Get Smart About Saving

Add the nightly business news and/or other business programs to your TV menu. It's to your advantage to know as much about the national economy as everyone else, so that when the talk at the office or at church turns to economic news, you'll be in the know. If it feels intimidating at first, create a ritual around this daily activity. Get a little aromatherapy going by lighting a scented candle, make yourself a nice cup of hot tea, and with pad and pencil at hand, take a few notes. Over time, you'll become familiar with the movers and shakers in the financial news.

Exercise Three: Visualize Your Savings Success

Think creatively to come up with visions of your savings success. Here are a few ideas to get you started:

- **Put an affirmation on the bathroom mirror** and practice saying it as you put on your makeup each morning. A good one is "I love to save and I'm great at it!"

- **Complete a deposit slip** with a large deposit on it, such as $10,000 or $100,000, and use it to visualize your upcoming prosperity.

- **Alter the balance** on your savings-account statement or investment-portfolio statement to the amount you'd like to have in the account. Use it to visualize abundance. For years, actor and comedian Jim Carrey visualized himself making $20 million per movie. Author Iyanla Vanzant asked her editors to alter a copy of *The New York Times* Bestseller List, placing her book, *In the Meantime*, at the top. Spurred by these motivational tools, both accomplished their goals. I've had clients visualize a zero balance on their Visa statements until it came true. Visualizing a goal can actually help you reach it.

 *Chapter Ten*

Prescription 7:
Get the Support and
Expert Advice You Need

I recently asked a client, "What resources and support were essential to the great success you achieved with your financial program?" She immediately replied, "You! You! You!" Of course, my ego would have loved to take full credit, but I know that's not the case. I did, however, enjoy reflecting for a moment on one of our sessions in the early days.

By our fourth meeting, I noticed a pattern that was developing with this sister. She would come into the office, sit down, open her copy of *The Basic Money Management Workbook,* and begin completing her spending plan for the upcoming month. I'd sit idly by, looking around the office, waiting for her to finish. After about fifteen or twenty minutes, she'd complete her totals and then direct her attention to me, ready to talk about her finances. Finally, I said to her, "Why don't you complete your spending plan at home? That way you don't waste your money having me sit here, and we can use our time together for discussion." She quickly replied, "Oh, no, you don't understand. I can't do this at home. It's too scary. Just having you here in the room helps me have the courage to put my expenses down on paper."

That timid client was Suzanne, the sister in Chapter Three who analyzed her family tree and went from $30,000 income to $160,000 income in seven years. Today, Suzanne acknowledges two other things that were critical to her success. "I did the work that you suggested and that helped me get clearer on what I wanted my life to look like—my goals and desires. Then I stayed mindful of the plan." She went on to describe how the work was a microcosm of the bigger picture and how writing down her spending daily kept her conscious of her money habits. Otherwise, she would lie to herself about how much was being spent. Suzanne continued, "Most important, I had a shift in my faith. The spiritual connection helped me realize that if I didn't do some unconditional walking with Spirit through every aspect of my life, accomplishing my dreams wasn't going to happen."

Suzanne's faith helped her keep her hope for positive outcomes alive even during the most difficult times. Because of her history of sexual abuse, reading a book entitled *Secret Survivors* by E. Sue Blume was key in getting in touch with the losses in her life, such as the loss of innocence and the loss of her childhood. She was able to figure out how this impacted her, and that opened the door to her financial breakthrough. "Overall, the process was simple, now that I can look back," Suzanne remarked. "But not easy," I interjected. "Yeah, thanks for adding that," she said. "Simple, but not easy."

In conversations with client after client who have successfully worked through their financial program with my assistance, a recurrent theme was the need to have faith in something outside of yourself in order to have hope for financial recovery. Each person recognized that they could only do so much—each had only so much control—before needing a source of strength to conquer the fear that plagues each of us who suffer from financial insecurity.

The Power of Forgiveness

Many blacks have been known to pray for a change in their financial condition, such as a new job, a raise, or maybe just a nice lottery jackpot! Some of these prayers are answered directly, but some have been answered indirectly through the power of forgiveness.

In her book *The Dynamic Laws of Healing*, Catherine Ponder discusses one of the greatest lessons we can learn in life. It is that we all have healing power and all healing is divine. She writes:

"If you have a problem, you have something to forgive. Anyone who experiences pain has a need to forgive. Anyone who finds himself in unpleasant circumstances has a need to forgive. Anyone who finds himself in debt has a need to forgive. Where there is suffering, unhappiness, lack, confusion or misery of any sort, there is a need to forgive."

Her statement "Anyone who finds himself in debt has a need to forgive" is correct. Often, financial problems may go unresolved because there is no direct connection between them and the need for forgiveness. But tracing back to when the problem first started, and what trauma or series of events may have taken place around that time, will often reveal the beginning of a downward spiral related to a forgiveness issue.

According to Ponder, "To forgive means to 'give for,' to 'replace' the ill feeling, to gain a sense of peace and harmony again. To forgive literally means to 'give up' that which you should not have held on to in the first place." Whether our problems manifest in physical, emotional, spiritual, or financial areas, we need to practice forgiveness.

Forgiving others is important as well as having others forgive us. But most important is forgiving ourselves. Here are some examples of forgiveness meditations that can help you work through negative experiences that may be preventing you from achieving your dreams:

I forgive everything, everyone, every experience, every memory of the past or present that needs forgiveness. I forgive positively everyone.

I am now forgiven by everything and everyone of the past and present that needs to forgive me. I am now positively forgiven by everyone.

The Healing Power of Meditation

Years ago, I remember seething with anger and obsessing about two people who were no longer in my life: my ex-husband and an ex-business associate. Much of my mental energy was spent on what I felt each of these people had done to me and how I didn't deserve to be treated that way. The obsession was so great that rarely an hour passed when I didn't have to consciously force the thought of one or the other from my mind. Expending so much energy on them, I hardly had the energy needed to get on with my life, let alone start a business and try to make it grow. I decided to try to get some peace by using a forgiveness meditation. I didn't want to forgive them, but I did want some relief from the madness, so I personalized the meditations by inserting their names and repeated them five times in the morning when I awoke and five times at night before I went to bed:

I fully and freely forgive you, (name). I release you and let you go. All ill feeling has been cleared up between us now and forever.

At some point during the evening of the fourth day of this ritual, I realized I had not thought of either of these individuals all day! To this day, it's a rare occasion when my mind drifts to these people who had previously drained me of so much valuable energy. As you already know, I went on to develop a successful financial counseling practice and ultimately to write this book. Not a bad way to get on with life!

My sister, Paula, has a great method for effectively dealing with uncertainty, negativity, and the challenges of day-to-day living. She works at staying "all prayed up." When she's "all prayed up," it's like a protective shield that emanates from her and around her. Nothing short of love can penetrate through. It's as if the negative darts and arrows that come at her from sources known and unknown just bounce right off.

When we stay "all prayed up," we are more peaceful within ourselves and we move through the world with a calm confidence and knowledge that all is well. We are not distracted if we don't have as much money as we would like, because we know the prosperity flow is taking place in our lives. We don't worry about a creditor phone call or letter from a collection agency, because we know we are taking the steps to assume financial responsibility for all our obligations. We stay focused on the plan that we developed with Divine guidance. We go into trust, and we take action when appropriate.

Finding Your Own Spiritual Path

The level and type of spirituality that we practice may change over the course of our lifetime—and that's okay. It's said that the family is the cornerstone of all civilization, and in most African American families, religious faith is a foundation laid in childhood—often in the Baptist church. As we get older, some of us begin the search for a spiritual message that resonates more closely with who we are as adults, given our changing beliefs and values. We must constantly stay attuned to what spiritual message resonates within us in order for the whole of our individual selves to feel satisfied and fulfilled.

During my life crisis in the late '80s, even though I had found a church that provided a message I could relate to and the fellowship that I desired, something was still missing. I remember having a conversation with my sister Barbara about prayer. Other than repeating the Lord's Prayer or saying, "God, I want this, I need that, or thank you for the other," I didn't know how to pray. For sure I knew my prayers didn't sound like the rousing, emotional exaltations that I remembered from the Baptist church, so obviously, I wasn't doing it right. Then Barbara said, "Just talk to God. Have a conversation with Him like you would with a person." This was many years before Neale Walsch's book *Conversations with God,* and at the time it seemed revolutionary to me. But when I tried it, it felt right and gave me peace because I felt like I was honestly connecting with the Almighty.

The point is, when connecting with Spirit you have to do it in a way that works best for you. It may sound somewhat different from how your friends and family do it, and that's okay. A source that I've found incredibly beneficial regarding prayers is Marianne Williamson's *Illuminata*. "The purpose of daily prayer," she says, "is the cultivation of a sense of the sacred. Sacred energy renews us." Her book of thoughts, prayers, and rites of passage covers a variety of topics and is written in everyday language. It tells you how to pray in a heartfelt and sincere manner.

Stay aware of what feels spiritually comfortable for you and what does not. You may connect better with a high-energy church environment, or maybe a more sedate, quiet worship environment is more to your liking. You may even go back and forth between the two, depending on your mood. There's nothing wrong with that. Stay true to yourself as you determine the best way to express gratitude for your blessings and the Divine source you turn to for support and sustenance.

Finding Support

As Dr. Brenda Wade said earlier, "There's nothing harder for a black woman than to reach out and get support." Often, that support requires a qualified therapist—a professional trained to objectively help us sort out and deal with issues that prevent our lives from working smoothly. African American sentiment has certainly changed over the years toward therapy. In the past, we resisted utilizing this sort of support because of trust issues resulting from having been historically betrayed. Our culture emphasized not telling other people our personal business, and therefore dirty secrets were perpetuated and kept within the family. A stigma of weakness was attached to any sort of counseling.

Now we sisters have learned that it is okay for us to seek help for our personal and financial problems. I view therapy as a very beneficial resource. It is an opportunity to sort things out with an objective person who can act as a sounding board. This person can provide reality checks for our thoughts and obsessive tendencies that are known to lead to spending excessively or other inappropriate uses of money. Have in mind a time frame for the support. That way you will not stay in therapy permanently, which can happen if you inadvertently transfer your addiction from overspending to overdependence on the therapist.

Even if you don't need a personal therapist, there are many other sources of support and financial advice that are available to you and can be extremely helpful in getting your money straight.

The Employee Assistance Department: A confidential consultation with a counselor at work can be of great benefit. Or ask trusted friends, family, or coworkers for referrals. Psychological counseling may also be available through your health-care provider. Many universities have an intern counseling service in their doctoral psychology program that provides therapy at a minimal cost under the supervision of a licensed psychologist. If you choose one of these resources, ask for the person you think you might best relate to with respect to race and gender. But if such an individual is not immediately available, select another person with whom you think you will be able to establish rapport.

A Financial Team: Coach, Accountant, Financial Planner, and an Attorney: If you like a customized one-on-one experience, you may want to organize your own financial team. Such a team can be made up of a financial coach, accountant, financial planner, and attorney. Just as a baseball coach maximizes the athletic production of his players, a financial coach suggests strategies for maximizing your financial production and can help you better understand your spending patterns, as I do with my holistic plan. An accountant makes sure you've correctly recorded your tax liability, expenses, and business revenues; a financial planner gives investment advice and helps you build wealth; an attorney can help you with legal matters and draft a will or living trust—a must even if you don't think you have assets. You do, whether they be the life insurance policy you have at work, your personal property, or your home. Just ask yourself what would happen if you died. Who would take care of your children? Who would take possession of your things?

Books, Tapes, and Videos: Bookstores are replete with books, tapes, and videos on money management. Browse through the personal finance section of more than one bookstore before making the selections that seem most suited to you. Prices may vary, and you can also look for markdowns and sale items.

Newspapers, Magazines, Radio, TV: Develop the habit of reading a good daily newspaper's business section. Most publish personal finance articles from which you can glean useful tips. As for magazines, *Black Enterprise, Essence,* and *Ebony* are among those that should be at the top of our lists. These African American–oriented publications have vital information on how to get your money straight and how to build wealth. As mentioned earlier, television business shows don't concentrate on finance for black people, but they do survey the overall economic scene and keep us abreast of fast-changing developments. If you like to listen to the radio, tune in to one of the nationally syndicated call-in shows on investing. Listen on your car radio as you go about your errands. Or try tucking a small portable in your pocket and listening to it with headphones while you do your housework. You can learn a lot while getting the dishes washed and the clothes laundered.

National Foundation for Consumer Credit: After you dial the toll-free crisis hotline for this organization at 800-388-2227, your call is automatically forwarded to a counseling center in your area. This nonprofit agency provides free counseling and low-cost debt management programs to people experiencing financial difficulties. Assistance can be provided in person, by telephone, or online.

Web Sites: Spend some time surfing the Web for sites that present financial information in a way that resonates best with your knowledge, interest, and personality. You'll find extensive networks such as BET.com or small sites like Cassandrasrevenge.com and smartsisters.com.

Public Financial Seminars: Keep your eyes peeled for financial seminars and conferences offered to the public as you read magazines and newspapers. These can be a good source of information presented in overview form. They can get you motivated, and later you can determine the resource that would be best to gain detailed knowledge. Be cautious, however, of seminars that offer expensive audiotapes for sale at the back of the room. You may find yourself drawn by a free or inexpensive seminar and then pressured to purchase a financial package for several hundred dollars.

Community College Courses: Contact your local community college or university for extension courses offered on personal finance. For minimal tuition you could take classes that address the fundamentals of money management in an environment designed for interaction and learning. One of my clients, after getting control of her finances through my program, moved on to obtaining a job in financial services and became so successful that she is now studying to become a certified financial planner.

Money Mentor or a Girlfriend Savings Support Group: Develop a mentor relationship with a friend or relative whose money management skills you admire and someone who might be willing to share their knowledge with you. Establish a regular time to check in with them—ten or fifteen minutes each week. Ask them financial questions and use them as a sounding board for financial decisions you have to make. Or invite three or four good friends to brainstorm and share ideas and resources for saving more money. For example: Buy clothes that can be washed instead of requiring dry cleaning. Meet once per quarter to provide support and share accomplishments.

Nontraditional Sources Are Good Too

Since *Girl, Get Your Money Straight!* is a financial book, the following list of resources and coping strategies may seem strange. I admit some are nontraditional. But mine is a holistic approach to money management, and the entirety of your being needs attention or its neglect could have a negative impact on your finances. For healing:

Communicate with your mate and set up a regular date night: When a friend of mine married, she and her husband created a blended family consisting of his son and her two daughters by previous marriages. Concentrating on full-time jobs and a nonstop household of three teenagers, they barely had time each day to say good morning and good night. Fearful of losing touch with the qualities that had brought them together in the first place, they scheduled a regular weekend coffee date. If you have young children, you may have to hire a babysitter in order to go out once a week. But the expense is worth it if you can carve out a couple of hours to reconnect in a relaxed atmosphere with your mate. Even if you don't have youngsters, your devotion to your careers may stand in the way of giving some focused time to each other.

Practice meditation: Start your quiet time by lighting a candle. If you want to put soft music on the radio, stereo, or CD player, that's good, but keep it barely audible and use it for background, not distraction. Start by repeating the Serenity Prayer, the Lord's Prayer, Psalm 23, or another favorite. Ask in a humble manner for guidance from a higher power in overcoming the doubts, fears, and anxieties you have about your money, your relationships, and the state of the world in general. Then sit silently with your eyes closed to allow your subconscious thoughts time to surface. Just as great ideas come to us when we're sleeping and we have trouble remembering them when we awake, workable solutions are formulating deep in our minds if only we quiet down long enough to become aware of them.

Consider deep-tissue bodywork: Memories of our life experiences are stored not only in our brains, but in our bodies as well. Bodywork practitioners work at the deeper levels of muscle tissue and help us explore these memories when they affect our overall wellness.

12-Step Programs: The 12-Step movement, started by Alcoholics Anonymous, has a saying: "Let us love you until you can love yourself." Recovery friendships are important, because they are with enlightened individuals who recognize, share, and accept our shortcomings. When we feel alone and isolated from others because of the shame of our finances, we can turn to others in our group who are battling similar personal demons. Below are some of the organizations whose members stand by to "welcome you to the club." (Look in your local telephone book for addresses and phone numbers.)

- **Debtors Anonymous,** for people with compulsive spending and debt problems. Visit www.debtorsanonymous.org/

- **Co-Dependents Anonymous,** for people with an inability to maintain functional relationships

- **Alcoholics Anonymous,** for people with drinking problems

- **Al-Anon,** for the families of people with drinking problems

- **Gamblers Anonymous,** for people with an addiction to gambling. Visit www.gamblersanonymous.org/

Exercise One: Do a Little Shopping—Church Shopping

If you feel a sense of spiritual deprivation or lack of spiritual connectedness, open your heart and your mind by taking one month to visit religious institutions of different denominations. You might ask friends if you can visit with them at their churches, synagogues, or mosques. Pick up the available literature and seek to get an understanding of the philosophy of each group. If you find one whose message clicks with you and the atmosphere makes you feel joyful yet comfortable, you'll know it's a community for you to get to know better in your search for spiritual nourishment.

Exercise Two: Forgive Yourself and Others

Step One: Everyone who considers him- or herself a part of the human race can look into their past and find situations and decisions they regret. Take some time and respond in writing to the following questions:

- What anger or hurt am I holding on to that is causing me to un-knowingly punish myself?
- What long-standing resentment is preventing me from taking advantage of opportunities to move forward in my life?
- How am I blocking myself from achieving greater financial success?
- What are three things I am willing to do to heal old wounds, reclaim my power, and get on with a peaceful, prosperous life?

Step Two: To begin healing from previous self-limiting experiences, repeat the following meditations mentioned earlier in this chapter five times first thing in the morning and five times the last thing at night:

> *I forgive everything, everyone, every experience, every memory of the past or present that needs forgiveness. I forgive positively everyone.*
>
> *I am now forgiven by everything and everyone of the past and present that needs to forgive me. I am now positively forgiven by everyone.*
>
> *I fully and freely forgive you, (name). I release you and let you go. All ill feeling has been cleared up between us now and forever.*

 *Part Three*

Beyond Getting
It Straight

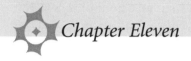*Chapter Eleven*

Building Wealth and
Funding Your Dreams

Living large and having great wealth is something we've all probably hoped for—whether we've verbally articulated these dreams or not. But we've also accepted the story of Prince Charming as nothing more than a fairy tale and have stopped expecting him to come to our rescue and provide us with a lifetime of financial security. Nevertheless, some of us have allowed ourselves to get caught up in the hype around the television program *Who Wants to Be a Millionaire?* and the fiasco around "who wants to marry one?" These are long shots, of course, and highly unlikely given the stiff competition to even participate. Even the economic boom of the 1990s has eluded many of us. The wealth gap between whites and nonwhites exists to an even greater extent than the gap between incomes. According to a survey conducted for the Federal Reserve, the median net worth in 1998 for non-white and Latino families was $16,400, versus an astounding $94,900 for white families. This means minorities have only 17.28 percent of the net worth of whites.

Why is there such a significant difference in wealth between the groups? A *Wall Street Journal* article of March 14, 2000, entitled "U.S. Racial Wealth Gap Remains Huge" points out, "Economists and researchers point to numerous reasons, including historical patterns of discrimination in wages, job opportunities and access to the credit needed to start a business. But differences in the way whites and non-whites invest appear also to be key. Minorities own homes at a much lower rate than whites and are far less likely to tuck their earnings into higher-risk investments such as stocks, which have generated a huge portion of the nation's new wealth over the 1990's." As strong-willed, intelligent, and financially capable sisters, we must begin to close the wealth gap and make some changes if we are to improve the legacy passed on to future generations. If we want to lead richer and fuller lives and see our dreams come true, we must actively work to build wealth by focusing on three key areas: investments, real estate, and entrepreneurship.

Creating Wealth Through Investments

Though the stock market may initially seem overwhelming, practically everybody can start investing in the market today. How? you ask. The answer is through your retirement program at work, which we discussed in Chapter Nine. The Ariel Mutual Funds/Schwab study states: "Since this type of account often is the gateway to investing, African Americans who are not participating in employee-sponsored plans are not gaining the same level of exposure to investment vehicles as are whites." This is evident given that just 67 percent of African Americans in the survey had money in employee-sponsored retirement programs compared to 72 percent of whites.

Even Shauna, the sister mentioned in Chapter Two who struggled for years with her $40,000 debt, had consistently contributed to her retirement plan. Shauna started making contributions at age thirty, and by age forty she had accumulated $225,000 (although she couldn't allow herself to enjoy the accomplishment because of the heavy debt burden). Over the last year, due to wise choices in investment options within her retirement plan, Shauna has increased her account by $100,000. It is now valued at $325,000!

Many of us put off wealth-building because we choose to focus on the wants and needs of the here and now. But you've heard it before— it's never too early and it's never too late to get started. Take my client, Rose. She didn't start contributing to her retirement plan until she was forty-two years old. By the time she started working with me eight years later at age fifty, she had accumulated $139,000 toward retirement. But she had also accumulated $32,000 in consumer debt, which consisted of an $18,000 home equity loan, a $7,000 loan against her retirement account, $5,000 in credit-card debts, and $2,000 in personal loans. With a mortgage of $148,000 on her $170,000 home, her $4,300 in monthly income never seemed to stretch far enough, and she always felt deprived. But Rose was determined to pay off her debt and be financially prepared for retirement. She developed a spending plan, tracked her spending consistently, rarely used her credit cards, and maintained a spiritual practice of affirmation, meditation, and visualization.

Writer, poet, and activist Rita Mae Brown said: "For you to be successful, sacrifices must be made. It's better that they are made by others, but failing that, you'll have to make them yourself." Rose made many sacrifices. She lost a little money when she sold her home, but by renting a flat that was close to her job she significantly cut her overhead by reducing her housing and transportation costs. She started contributing the maximum to her retirement account, and began building a savings cushion as she paid off her debts. Today, at age fifty-four, Rose has $300,000 in retirement funds and $4,200 in a savings cushion. Out of a seemingly dire situation, she has started to build substantial wealth that will help see her through her retirement years in style.

I have a special message for all of the young sisters in their mid-twenties who are reading this book right now. Many of you are recently out of college and embarking on your chosen careers. You're finally out of school and, I'm sure, saying, "Thank you, Lord," because you're just starting to make some real money. You might have the mind-set that you're entitled to spend money because you've worked hard through school and there will be plenty of time to save in the future. Well, you're right. There is a lot of time for you to plan for retirement. But time is on your side *right now*, because there's an opportunity for you to build *incredible* wealth during your lifetime. You can enjoy a life of ease, comfort, *and* "early" retirement with financial security if you're willing to sacrifice a little bit to start now.

A Little Bit Goes a Long Way

Let's take Teri, for example—a twenty-two-year-old honors graduate of Howard University. Smart and talented, Teri was hired immediately for her first position as an administrative assistant for a systems technology company in the Washington, D.C., area. Her starting salary of $31,000 was impressive and seemed like a large amount of money. But even with a roommate and a little help from her parents, who paid her car insurance, it still didn't seem to be enough to even consider saving, let alone put away for retirement. But let's say Teri was willing to make a bit of a sacrifice and save a minimum of $100 per month. That could be accomplished through simply buying fewer CDs each month, forgoing a couple of dinners out, skipping one movie, cutting down on the Jamba Juice, and purchasing one less outfit.

Now, here's the exciting news. Teri's $100 deduction from her paycheck, if started at age twenty-five, would add up to $48,000 by age sixty-five if she put it into savings. But invested with a 12 percent annual rate of return, it would equal a whopping $1,188,242 at retirement! However, if she waits until age thirty-five to start her $100-per-month contribution, she would have only $352,991 at age sixty-five. Imagine that—$835,251 less available at retirement because she waited ten years to get started. And don't even think about waiting until age forty-five to start—she'd have only $99,915 at retirement and would have lost $1,088,327 by putting it off.

I was recently encouraged by a conversation with two impressive elementary-school teachers—my niece Stephanie and her friend

Vanessa. Both are recent graduates of Spelman College and have already started saving for their retirement. When asked what motivated them to begin so early, both explained how they had parents who were super savers and investors, as well as aunts and uncles who encouraged them. "Aside from that," remarked Stephanie, "I knew my parents would kill me if I didn't!" She later admitted that growing up in a household with my sister Doris and brother-in-law Darrell, where there was a strong consciousness about the importance of saving, was a significant factor.

Unfortunately, these two young sisters are not typical twenty-somethings. They are quick to say how they feel their generation lives for the here and now, getting motivated to save only for a fancy car for "show" purposes. "Society has corrupted us," one said, describing how young people today go for the diamond and gold jewelry and designer clothing they see athletes and hip-hop musicians wearing. "Even the young parents of our students—many of whom live in subsidized housing—dress their children in designer clothes when they should be saving for the kids' college education."

Investing for the Long Term

If the mere thought of investing money in the stock market fills you with apprehension and terror, you're not alone. About 56 percent of African Americans, compared to 35 percent of whites, believe investing in stocks is just like gambling. Even though lots of black folks will play the lottery every week, they are afraid to risk putting the same amount of money into the stock market.

"Nobody ever got rich simply by working a job," is an often-heard saying. The truth is, to really make money, we must own businesses outright or at least have a piece of ownership in them. When you own stocks, you do just that—when you purchase shares, you are purchasing a piece of the company. Because your money grows or diminishes depending on the success of the business, it's a riskier method of building funds for the future. But there's a much higher rate of return, and if you pick your stocks wisely, your assets can grow much more rapidly than it would in a savings account. Within the last few years, it's been easy to get caught up in the hype of the capital markets given the growth and the ease with which anyone can now buy and sell stocks using the Internet and Web sites such as E*TRADE.

Some of us have hesitated to get in on the action, however, because we think we need $5,000 or $10,000 just to get started. You don't. What we do need is to start wherever we are and learn more as we go along. All of the following investment options involve stocks, so here are some ways you can begin to create your investment portfolio:

Stocks: There are two types of stocks. Common stock entitles the owners to receive regular dividends (if declared by the board of directors), to vote at annual shareholder meetings, or to authorize other persons to vote on their behalf. Preferred stock usually has no voting rights, pays limited but specified dividends, and has priority claim over common stock to earnings (dividends) and assets (liquidation value) of the corporation.

Investment Clubs: This is a great way to enhance your knowledge about investing. Most clubs average ten to twelve people, with each person investing about $50 per month. Members share the responsibility for education and research of stocks, and purchases are made based on a consensus. You can also increase your individual net worth by applying the information learned in the club to your personal purchases. For information on how to start an investment club, contact the National Association of Investors Corporation at (877) 275-6242, or visit their Web site, www.better-investing.org. Or visit the Web site for Coalition of Black Investors (COBI) at www.cobinvest.com. Their mission is to enhance financial literacy and promote saving and investing by African Americans.

Employee Stock Purchase Plan (ESOP): This is a stock ownership plan where employees can purchase shares in their company's stock.

Shares can be purchased through a stock-purchase option, or through a company-sponsored 401K plan.

Dividend Reinvestment Plans (DRIPs): Almost nine hundred companies offer dividend reinvestment plans. DRIPs allow current shareholders to purchase stock directly from the company, bypassing brokers and commissions. Most of these plans provide the investor with an opportunity to buy additional shares of stock with the cash dividends paid by the company at no charge.

Mutual Funds: These investment companies raise money by selling shares to the public. This pool of money is invested in stocks, bonds, options, and money-market instruments. The portfolio is then professionally managed, with securities bought and sold at the discretion of the manager.

Mutual funds are another way to gradually build wealth with minimal investment. Loretta, a thirty-three-year-old social worker, started her mutual fund with $250 and committed to add $100 a month by automatic deduction from her checking account. She chose a growth-and-income fund with moderate risk and then because of a busy work schedule focused her attention on other things. She only casually glanced at her statements when they came in the mail. It was over three years later before she realized her mutual fund averaged a meager 12.66 percent annual return during a bull market when others were making money hand over fist. The average return for the Standard & Poor's 500 for the same five-year period had been 22.60 percent.

Frustrated with herself for the years of neglect, Loretta started talking with friends and family members who had investments. She read fund prospectuses and financial magazines and compared the annual rate of returns for various mutual funds. Soon she decided on an aggressive fund with an average annual return for three years of 51.51 percent and five years of 40.33 percent. Loretta added another $3,000 to her $4,600 account and moved the money to the new fund. Amazingly, she transferred her money at the perfect time—just as the fund was taking off. In just seven months she has seen an 82 percent return on her investment and watched her account grow to almost $14,000!

Real Estate: The Old Reliable

The Ariel Mutual Funds/Schwab study further found that African Americans have a strong "culture of conservatism" when it comes to investing. As a result, real estate is viewed as the best investment by 39 percent of African Americans compared to just 30 percent of whites. It's considered the best because it's less risky, it will never go down in value, you can use it to earn rental income, you can borrow on the equity, and it's tangible—you can see it and touch it. If you are most comfortable with real estate, you should consider buying an income-generating property. For example, a new homeowner might consider a duplex or triplex as a first property. The additional rental income can be very beneficial and possibly allow the unit to pay for itself.

Knowing African Americans are still discriminated against by banks and other financial institutions causes black women to be fearful and intimidated by the process of purchasing property. Each encounter is approached with an expectation of rejection. The fear of being rejected—even when we know our credit is squeaky clean—is scary and often is the reason many black women wait so long to purchase a home. A thirty-four-year-old friend of mine was once asked by an acquaintance who was aware that she had a well-paying, stable job, "If you don't own a home, what are you doing with all of your money?" It was something that she hadn't really thought about, because for her it seemed unlikely that an unmarried African American woman would be able to accomplish such a task on her own. Before the year was out, my friend had purchased an attractive three-bedroom brick home with a full finished basement. All she needed to know was that it was possible and that it made sense for her to do it. And, in fact, it was a great investment for the future.

Lack of education regarding the home-buying process is also problematic. Some women think they need to save forever for a 20 percent down payment because that's the only type of mortgage loan available. Rose, who was mentioned earlier in this chapter because she started her retirement saving at age forty-two, took advantage of a couple of other options available for home purchase. She and a longtime girlfriend decided to purchase a beautiful $500,000 four-unit apartment building. Rose made a $25,000 loan against her retirement account (which had accumulated $300,000) and used it as a down payment for the property. Her friend matched the $25,000 and they used it as a 10 percent down payment for a 90 percent loan to buy the building. Rose's only debt—besides her portion of the mortgage—is the 7.8 percent interest on the retirement account loan that in effect is being paid to herself. This way she didn't have to use any of her retirement funds and acquired a great piece of property in the process.

Today, Rose is a very happy homeowner living in one of the units with a great view of the Berkeley Hills. By contributing to her retirement account consistently, she is not only building financial security, she is accumulating the resources to make another major real estate purchase in the future and continue expanding her wealth. There are many different opportunities in the real estate arena that can suit individual needs. With a multifamily dwelling you can sometimes live free, and eventually the building pays for itself. Co-ops and condos are another place to start. A word of caution, though. Be sure to do your homework and take appropriate legal precautions when deciding to form a partnership for real estate purchases.

Entrepreneurship

A brotherfriend of mine, who had achieved great success in the corporate world and consistently earned a six-figure salary, once said to me, "I really admire your accomplishment as an entrepreneur. I don't think I could ever do that because of the lack of security and fluctuating income." At the time, I had been in business about five years, working hard to establish myself, and hadn't really thought about how much of an accomplishment it was. But it's true. And many women of color are stepping out on faith and becoming entrepreneurs. Between 1987 and 1996, businesses owned by women of color increased 135 percent.

But not everybody is cut out to be in business for themselves—even though they've achieved success as employees and know the inner workings of their companies. Of course, there's nothing wrong with being an employee. One can certainly, over time, accrue enough money to provide financial security from your wages. However, it's abundantly clear that profits made in businesses are not proportionately passed down to employees. So it makes sense that in order to be entitled to greater profits generated by companies, we need to own them.

One thing about being an entrepreneur is that the "buck stops with you" *and* "the buck starts with you." Your initiative and discipline are the major determining factors in whether there is money available to pay the rent when it's due. It's not about just going to the job and doing enough to get by so you can pick up a paycheck on the first and fifteenth of the month. But if you're motivated and proactive and creative enough to take full charge of your financial well-being and devote yourself to your business body and soul, becoming an entrepreneur is an excellent way to generate more income and grow your net worth.

We Must Promote Ourselves

We've all heard of Madam C. J. Walker. The first self-made female millionaire is an inspiration for all entrepreneurs. This is so not just because of her incredible accomplishment, but because she started her business in 1905 and became a millionaire in 1919, with over three thousand sisters working together and selling her hair care products. Madam Walker's great-great-granddaughter, A'lelia Bundles, reminds us that she was a woman who experienced challenges, just like us. She got married, had children, raised a family, and experienced a divorce.

Bundles delights in sharing a story about how Madam Walker, after being denied an opportunity to officially speak at a National Negro Business League Conference, seized the moment and said, "I started out in the cotton fields. Then I was promoted to the washer tub. Then I was promoted to the cook kitchen. Then I promoted myself." Madam C. J. Walker enjoyed incredible success and even built her factory on her own land.

As African American women, we must promote ourselves to prosperity and wealth. Without argument, we are strong, courageous, resourceful, and resilient. The strength that it took to survive the middle passage and subsequent years of slavery has become a part of our genetic makeup. We're less likely to sit back and wait for someone to give us something and are more likely to do what it takes to make things happen.

We often marvel at the accomplishments of Oprah Winfrey—as well we should. She has done a phenomenal job of creating an extensive business empire. But we should also look around our communities and recognize other successful black women whose paths we've crossed. In 1998 I met Elana Turner James, a thirty-three-year-old, high-energy sister who really impressed me. Elana grew up in a Chicago housing project, the daughter of two loving parents who owned a small convenience store. The store didn't make much money because of the amount of credit extended to neighborhood patrons. But Elana worked for her father—that is, until he fired her because she was undependable and irresponsible.

As a teenager, Elana was intent on taking a trip to the Bahamas that her father wouldn't pay for, so she took a job at a McDonald's restaurant as a cashier with plans to work there only a few weeks. Surprisingly, she loved it and worked at the company for seventeen years before purchasing her own store two years ago. Today, Elana is a single parent and proud owner/operator of two successful McDonald's franchises in the Washington, D.C., area.

During that seventeen-year period, her master plan wasn't always evident to others. Elana heard comments like "You aren't making any money. Why don't you get a *real* job?" When Elana continued to work at McDonald's after earning two bachelor's degrees and a master's, her mother said, "After all this college education, you're still at McDonald's. Have you lost your mind?" But Elana was undeterred. She was able to give her mother adequate assurance that a plan was in place, and Mom eventually sighed, "Okay, baby." Now her proud parents are heard to say, "Could you call *The Washington Post* and ask them to send fifty copies of the article they did on you last week so we can pass them out at church?"

Certainly, buying a franchise is not the easiest way to become an entrepreneur. In fact, it can be quite costly. Elana's first franchise cost

$490,000, of which she needed 25 percent down plus a $45,000 franchising fee. But with a little ingenuity, she managed it. She took advantage of profit-sharing opportunities while she worked at McDonald's, and as she puts it: "I was a bonusin' sista! I knew how to make that money!" She earned her bonuses by turning out record volume while managing stores for other owners. She also watched her bosses. "He gets a new Benz every year," she said about one man. "I knew that if I was making that kind of money for him, I could be making it for myself." Elana refrained from buying new outfits and new cars as she earned her bonuses. "I love nice shoes and handbags," she said. "But I saved, saved, saved my money. It's okay to buy yourself trinkets to stay motivated, but learn to window-shop and take a miserly friend with you. Someone who's known to be cheap."

Elana's strategy paid off, and her "junkyard dog tenacity" continues to help her excel in business.

☼ The Sister's Declaration of Financial Independence ☼

Every sister that I've mentioned in this book has made a personal commitment not only to get her money straight but to move beyond that triumph to create wealth for fun and financial serenity. I invite you to do what they have done. Today, right here, right now, decide that you will take the following steps and declare your intentions to the world:

I, _____, hereby declare that I am committed to getting my money straight and that I will:

- **Draw on the courage and wisdom of our elders** and use what's appropriate for our modern day and time. I know I come from a strong people, Africans who transformed bondage and created much of what is known as American culture today. My ancestors knew how to make something out of nothing, and my grandparents and parents did too. I will use those skills today to live below my means, create a little extra, and use that extra to grow my personal wealth.

- **Be grateful for life's experiences and learn from them**. For instance, before I consider taking out a consolidation loan, I will get some expert help to figure out how my debt got so out of control in the first place. I'll look back on my period of financial crisis and be grateful for the lessons I brought with me from that time. I will learn from my mistakes and be less likely to repeat them.

- **Get quiet and assess my goals and objectives**. I will take a few hours out at the beginning of the year, or, better yet, as soon as I finish reading this book to visualize a blank canvas and begin to mentally paint a picture of how I want the next five to ten years to look. I will ask myself what my burning desire is, whether I've picked the right goal, how I'll keep that goal in front of me every day, what action I'll take to achieve it, how I'll achieve balance in my life while pursuing the goal, what benchmarks I'll establish to judge my progress, and whether I've established a set of spiritual practices to put me in touch with my Higher Self.

- **Put my plan in writing**. This is probably the most important step I can take toward getting my money straight. My document will not be a budget that makes me feel deprived. Instead, my spending plan is a positive declaration of my intentions. It means *I* am deciding how I'm going to manage *my* income. It helps me identify what I need to do to maintain a quality life. It's a blueprint for getting my financial house in order.

- **Monitor my plan by tracking**. The best spending plan is useless unless I follow through. Being able to account for my finances is important. There are a number of ways to accomplish this task. The sooner I start, the sooner I will get a true picture of what I am doing with my money.

- **Take time to analyze and modify**. After several months, I will begin to see my spending patterns. I may be spending much more on hair care, snacks, or even cappuccino than I realized. Once I compare my actual spending habits with what I want to spend my money on, I will be in a position to modify my pattern to move in the direction I want to go.

- **Show gratitude and give back**. When I take control of my financial life, I will pause a moment to do something kind for someone else. As my money management improves, I may find I have more cash flow each month. I will take a portion of that discretionary income and give it to my favorite charities.

God Bless You

As I close this book, I'd like to share a few more thoughts that I hope you will take with you on the journey to getting your money straight:

Self-acceptance without judgment and criticism is essential. To begin financial healing, it's crucial to let go of negative energy by forgiving yourself and anyone else you might want to blame for the financial bind you are in.

Take better care of yourself, not by spending more money on self-indulgent pampering if you are already financially strapped, but, rather, by not beating up on yourself anymore. Don't berate yourself for past mistakes. Instead, stand tall and decide that you're going to grab this second chance and make good on it this time around.

Start focusing on your heart. Be attuned to its messages. Learn to pray or meditate from the heart on whatever force outside yourself you believe in. Remember the words of Marianne Williamson: "The purpose of daily prayer," she says, "is the cultivation of a sense of the sacred. Sacred energy renews us." As my sister Paula says, stay "all prayed up" and full of love and peace. Know when to say when, then let go and let God.

By following the steps in *Girl, Get Your Money Straight!,* I found financial stability that led to financial security and ultimately to a degree of financial freedom. And with that freedom I have now afforded myself the opportunity to write another chapter in my book of life. I recently expanded my financial counseling business and moved back to Detroit. Why? Because by staying in touch with my feelings and desires, I have decided after twenty-four years in California that I want to spend some quality time with my aging parents while I can. We are having a wonderful time going out to lunch and doing things together—many times just the three of us—without my siblings or nieces or nephews. It's our special time. I'm looking forward to many more days of shopping and getting my hair done with Mom and golfing with Dad.

Traveling between the two cities is a dream come true for me, and I plan to enjoy it until I decide I want to do something else. Please join me and many other African American women in the quest to get and keep our money straight. Be in control of the direction of your life and be blessed.

Index